The Lean Guide to Digital Advertising

HOW TO IDENTIFY, TEST AND BUILD YOUR
GROWTH ENGINE
(SECRET TITLE: AD TECH FOR ENTREPRENEURS)

Brent W. Halliburton

Halliburton & Sons
BETHESDA, MD

Halliburton & Sons
7800 Cindy Lane
Bethesda, MD 20817
www.brenthalliburton.com

Book Layout ©2013 BookDesignTemplates.com

Ordering Information:
Quantity sales. Special discounts are available on quantity purchases by corporations, associations, and others. For details, contact the "Special Sales Department" at the address above.

The Lean Guide to Digital Advertising/ Brent Halliburton. —1st ed.
ISBN 978-0-6926074-9-7

Contents

*I would like to take a moment to thank
my delightful and supportive wife.*

CHAPTER 1

Introduction

Chances are you have already failed. Failure is what startups do. We fail. Repeatedly. But it is not over yet. This book represents my attempt to make sure you do not fail once too often. Start-ups are an experiment, experiments fail. If it was easy, everyone would do it.

The dimensions of failure are many but they can be boiled down to the two dimensions upon which a business is based: innovation and selling. If you aren't innovating, your products become terrible over time. It could be supply chain innovation or it could be inventing the iPhone. You have to innovate to win. The vogue thing to talk about today is innovation. There are lots of ways to innovate and they are necessary to be successful. But that is not all.

The other source of failure is, in many instances, far more common but less understood and more insidious. No one buys your product. But I am not talking about poor customer development. Customer development is part of innovating - you have to find a novel solution to a problem people actually have. Let us assume you are past that: People need your product. You innovated to solve a problem that customers have. The challenge you cannot overcome is the terrible job you did selling it. Many technology entrepreneurs hate to be selling. People think like this because when most people talk about selling, they are talking about "sales people". A world where developing skills involve reading books like "Tricks To Confuse Purchasing Agents" or "1000 Ways To Close A Deal". The pre-emptive close: "So would you like to pay now or should we invoice you?" Things that non-sales people hear about and it makes them feel dirty even knowing that the idea exists. Selling is for people whose product isn't good enough. It's dirty. It's not the last resort, because we would never resort to that.

Further, in our modern world, conventional wisdom is that there is no sales person. The sales person is "in the cloud". You hear stories about Mint and Instagram where they just build a great product, have some great blog ("Content marketing! Woo-hoo!"), do some "growth hacking" and win. But Peter Thiel recently said, "Most businesses actually get zero distribution channels to work. Poor distribution--not product--is the number one cause of failure.[1]" Heed the guy who has made billions of dollars starting tech companies.

You read about people on Hacker News saying "I changed this button color from blue to green and made $10,000".

I am here to tell you that the reason people read that post about button colors on Hacker News is not because they will learn anything, but because it is an outlier. They are like super models. The real world isn't like that. Hacker News is TMZ for entrepreneurs, bringing you the sexy, beautiful people of the startup world. Don't quit your job and move to Hollywood and think you will be just like them.

I am here to tell you that there is a better way. People that build better mouse traps are a dime a dozen. Nikola Tesla invented the alternating current electrical model, a superior electric method to direct current, but Thomas Edison outsold him and the result is North America is a DC world. For every Instagram, there are 20 companies that made Instagram and died. I could tell you the names of some of them, but you never heard of them because they never sold. You do not want to build a company with a plan to never figure out revenue. That is relying on the ever-popular "hope" strategy and one should never rely on that.

Instagram and Dropbox and AirBnB are exceptions to the rule. You can't build a business patterned after outliers. In the real world, the world you are building your business for, revenue does not magically appear. You have to do the work. For every Waze, there are 100 companies that do the same thing and only their mom visits their site. #truth

While Customer Development has become increasingly well-documented and allows lean start-ups to feel like they have a data driven plan for developing a product that the market desires[1], the same is not true for selling it. Selling takes work and without it, customer development will not work. Allow me to illustrate one example: One of the great concepts of running lean revolves around testing ideas.

Unfortunately, when a test fails it is not clear if the idea is poor or the test was flawed. Did no one click the ad because the product is not valued or because the ad was terrible? Did no one sign up because the product is undesirable or because the sign up experience was a bad user experience? That terrible ad and that bad user

---

1. Don't get me wrong: Customer development is great. Steven Blank, Eric Ries and the science of the lean startup have brought new discipline to the art of starting companies and building innovation. When I describe my last start-up, I tell people that I did 70% of The Four Steps to the Epiphany and if there was one thing I would do next time, it would be to do 100%.

experience are poor sales at work. They took your good product and your customer development work and blew it sky high.

Every year, lean startups fail because the answers are difficult to discern. Startups pivot when their founding idea was strong yet their initial marketing was weak. Without fixing their marketing, they continue to pivot until they run out of money. They take perfectly good ideas, test them, watch the market hate their marketing, confuse that with thinking that the market hates their product, and throw everything away. Alternately, they choose to believe that the test is wrong and place blind faith in a flawed product, abandoning the value of lean testing.

Lean Start-ups know that this is a risk, but they don't have a way to mitigate this risk. Fortunately, the world of digital advertising has, unbeknownst to lean startups, spent the last decade building a body of knowledge converting this into a science. Computational advertisers know what landing pages convert the best, what banners convert the best, how to test a phrase, and more broadly, how to build what I call "scalable revenue".

Some revenue isn't scalable: You hit on a keyword in Google that brings you 10 customers per day that buy your products for $10. That's great, but do you know what is great about that keyword? Do you know how to find more keywords just like it? Can you make targeted keywords on Google scale to $1,000 per day?

You have a great blog post that reaches number one on Hacker News. That is great, but you need a system for producing popular posts on Hacker News or your business is like the movie business. It's a hit business with random outcomes and high variability. Lean Startups know that there is a need for more predictability than this. The goal of being lean is to decrease randomness and variability. We need to build a machine that lets us turn the crank and make money pop out. Sometimes this machine is a pump that needs to be primed, and that is ok. If we have to put a five dollar bill into the machine to get ten dollars out, and you know with absolute certainty that every time you put in five dollars, ten dollars pops out five minutes later, that is a great machine. That is a machine that we can use. That is scalable revenue.

There is a real-time auction of attention happening right now. You can participate in this auction and use the digital advertising ecosystem to more effectively experiment and build revenue streams. Every second, billions of people are looking at things on the Internet, offering their attention and making it available to publishers and advertisers. Each of these people have attributes: currently reading content about finance, in the past they have looked at content about sports, etc. These attributes have value to advertisers and advertisers are actively bidding on them on the Internet today. Each page request that contains an advertisement begins an instantaneous auction for your attention that requires dozens of advertisers to determine exactly the value of your attention to them and respond with an appropriate advertisement in 100 milliseconds.

I have been on both sides of this table. I have founded three companies and sold two on my terms (third is still active). I have built companies using lean start-up techniques and I have built them without (that is harder). I started companies that generated millions in revenue. I was early in at companies that went from $1 million to $100 million. I have worked in digital advertising for a decade, including running Aol and Advertising.com's New Product Development group and managing product for Verve Mobile, a large mobile advertising network (albeit very, very small when we started). I know what you need to do. And I am ready to give you everything.

All you have to do are two things.

One:

Be willing to get close to the iron. That is a euphemism I use with all my tech friends that you can't be scared to look at some code, to go get on your computer and geek out, to be ready to fool around with the server. I'm not a programmer, so you don't need to be, but you can't be scared of code. To win, we have to have an information advantage. Knowledge is power and knowledge comes from being close to the iron. All of the action is happening inside the machine. We can't be afraid to get in there and learn how the machine works.

You are not well-served by being a person that just hangs out at 10,000 feet and doesn't really understand what's going on. You need to know!

Two:

Learn to love math. You might think you don't like math, but math is not just fun, it is important. Advertising today is about quantitative analysis. Just like Lean Startups are about testing and science, Lean Advertising requires math. Computational advertising is about finding mathematical inequities and exploiting them for gain. We should do that because that gain is your gain.

Building repeatable marketing success is not about hoping for a magic creative breakthrough and inventing "Subservient Chicken[2]", it is about finding pockets of value and capturing them. That takes math. To make money in the digital world, you have to want to know if you want to buy 250 clicks for $0.40 each, knowing that those 250 clicks generate $100.00 in revenue. (Eh, it's a break-even proposition: 250 * 0.4 = 100)

I am going to talk about measuring things. I am going to say measurement so many times you will be sick of the word. Building a growth engine requires measuring what you do to know what works and what doesn't. We are going to measure all day long.

In order to give you great advice, I have to understand you and I have to know the answers to your questions. We have to be talking about the same thing. For the purpose of this book, I am assuming that you and I have a lot in common:

- I am assuming that you are a small business (sub $20 million in revenue), probably early stage
- I am assuming that you are doing this to acquire additional customers.
- I am assuming your product is good enough. More specifically, in the language of lean, I am assuming that you have a strong minimum viable product ("MVP"). By this, I mean that it doesn't do a lot of things, but for its target market, your product has at least one amazing feature that really meets their needs. If your product doesn't have an "Aha" moment inside of it then it probably isn't ready for you to share with the world.

Note that these assumptions don't differentiate between businesses that have raised money and those that haven't. Even if you have raised a lot of money, the focus has to be on efficiency. If you pivot later, you will regret every nickel you spent now on things that didn't bring you one step closer to winning. Similarly, it is good to work from the assumption that any marketing tactic that you try may not work. That is why we emphasize testing, metrics, and attribution as the core of the business.

Radio and television are not covered here because digital will be more valuable for the first fifty million dollars in revenue for your business. Digital is the starting point because it is easy to test, easy to connect successful conversions to spend and one can rapidly dial spend (and associated revenue) up and down. Radio and TV are techniques for after product market fit and acceleration.[2]

I will walk you through every aspect of building a digital scalable revenue machine. Furthermore, I will tell you everything there is to know about the digital advertising ecosystem. To leverage it, you have to understand it and understanding it is complex. I will walk through some of the history of digital advertising as well, because much of the complexity comes from how it has evolved from simple beginnings. If you know the simple beginnings and why it became more complex, then grasping the nuances of the modern day are simpler. When I first started working in digital advertising, I had spent more than a decade building web sites, but I found myself woefully unprepared to actually help people make money. This is the book that I wish I had then to explain to me why things are the way they are, how things work, and how to use all of that to my advantage.

It doesn't matter if you are part of the digital advertising industry, a start-up driving to one million dollars in revenue, an early stage business getting to ten million dollars, or someone that works at an agency or consultancy in this industry, everyone needs a deeper understanding of how to make this multi-billion dollar industry work for them.

Notes

1. http://25iq.com/2014/05/17/a-dozen-things-ive-learned-about-marketing-distribution-and-sales/

---

2. Or for trained professionals. If that is your thing, go crazy. Raise money from the QVC lady on Shark Tank.

2. http://subservientchicken.com/

CHAPTER 2

Results, Response & Value

Different businesses need different types of growth engines. There are four primary engines that business use to fuel their growth and they each are most appropriate for specific kinds of situations.

- Growth by brute force - Sales People
- Growth by machines - SEO
- Growth by people - Virality
- Growth by cash - Paid Acquisition

Each of these approaches can be matched to business models as business models have different requirements. Also, many businesses will find that their model encourages a mixture of growth techniques, but most business find that there is a dominant sales engine that really takes their business to the next level.

Companies like Oracle do a lot of different marketing activities, but they have grown through sheer brute force: They have an amazing sales force that sells their multi-million dollar databases one customer at a time. For About.com, that growth was growth by machines - having great content made Google love them. Google then directed billions of consumers to the About.com web site. Facebook used a different strategy; they were able to create an incredibly strong network effect by encouraging members of the community to refer new members. This "growth by people" strategy has made them the largest web site in the world. Finally, companies like Amazon and eBay pursue paid marketing strategies where third parties such as Google show ads for their products, resulting in tremendous revenue.

Growth by brute force is hiring sales people to sell your products. Let's be honest, if your product costs more than $2,000, this is a pretty good way to go. If you are selling something that is a sophisticated purchase with a complex sales cycle, you probably need someone to manage it. This isn't "Internet-scalable" - sales only grow as fast as you can staff your sales organization - hence we won't be discussing it in this book, but if your product needs a sales organization, you need to build it. The things in this book will be tools for lead generation. You need to find people for the sales organization to talk to and many of these people can be found using the alternate growth strategies.

Growth by machines is the best strategy for organizations that have active communities on their site and/or create a lot of content. Wikipedia is one of the most visited sites in the world because the sheer amount of content resident in Wikipedia and the frequency with which it is referenced has caused Google and Bing to both rely heavily on it for many different search results. The end product of that interaction is that it is one of the most common results returned by internet searches for information and millions of consumers visit Wikipedia via search engines every day for answers to their questions. When I founded Cogmap, a wikipedia for organization charts, I met briefly with Josh Kopelman, a partner at First Round Capital and one of the most brilliant marketing minds in the world. He told me that at least 80% of

Cogmap traffic should be Google searches. He appreciated the importance of winning the search engine wars with a business model such as these. The challenge to this strategy is that it can take a non-trivial amount of time to test the effect of changes. This makes it less practical for start-ups that are in the earliest stages of product growth testing.

Growth by people is one of the most well-known strategies because these products tend to be some of the finest products you can find. To grow powered by word of mouth requires an incredible product that is highly tuned to engage virality. Most social networks operate this way, so it has been the growth engine of choice for platforms like Twitter and Instagram. Once again, this method can be incredibly effective over the long term, but in the early stages of being lean, it is difficult because the assumption is that the product has been polished to a fine sheen. Unless the products essence is built on a referral engine, the network effect of these strategies is limited. Most start-ups engaged in this type of challenge spend a lot of time talking about "the chicken and the egg". They need users to create value and drive referrals, but they need referrals to acquire users.

Finally, growth by cash or paid acquisition of customers is one of the most common approaches for sales and this is the area that we will spend the most time talking about. While using cash to grow sounds terrible, trading one dollar for two dollars is a great, great, great way to grow. Building an effective growth engine that arbitrages cash is among the most scalable ways to grow: Everyone wants money. Using cash to grow is how Coca-Cola works, Nike works, and most other large companies you are familiar with. Even Google pays hundreds of millions of dollars per year to organizations such as Mozilla to make sure that their search engine is featured prominently in the Firefox browser. When you are paid for the use of your product, your product has a clear and well-defined model for understanding the value of customers to your business. You can use this to arbitrage marketing spend to grow your company. This strategy is very effective because it can be turned on and off easily, it can scale very well, and it becomes more powerful over time: as marketing dollars and the value of consumers grows to the business, the business unlocks the ability to spend more to acquire customers via growth.

Measure Outcomes

People generally think of measuring the result as the last thing you do, but I am going to make it the first thing I talk about because thinking about the desired outcome is the starting point both physically and mentally. Getting an analytical framework erected to understand the effectiveness of what you are doing is not just the actual first thing you do, it is a state of mind that tells you what to do and how to do it as you launch your ideas.

You make New Year's Resolutions at the start of the year. You figure out your goals and set up an infrastructure to measure them. We have goals because otherwise we don't know what to do.

Let's talk about making New Year's Resolutions for a digital experience: When you put up a web site or build an app, you need to get your analytics straight. I will talk a lot more about exactly how to do this later, but the important thing to know now is that you need to get it done. Before anyone comes to visit your awesome thing, you want to make sure that you are capturing the digital bread crumb trail they leave behind. Why would you let good data come to your organization and not look at it? Understanding the what, how, and why of your customers is what playing the game is about, so analytics is one of the first things you think about when you build a new product.

If the definition of a start-up is a series of experiments to discover a scalable and repeatable business model, then being thoughtful about understanding what you are trying, what the expected outcome should be, and what learnings you will generate to drive future experimentation is critical to the success of your project. A scientist controls his experiments to ensure that he could repeat them again in the future. If your experiment is not replicable, the experiment has no value.

This is how direct marketers think about their job, so the mindset we are adopting as entrepreneurs is the direct response mindset. We don't want to spend money on experiments that aren't designed to help us acquire customers. We don't spend money on activities that make people "like" us more (unless that makes them turn into customers). That is branding and branding is for people that have money to waste. We don't care if you haven't heard of us if you are not the kind of person that should be a customer. (Sorry Mom!) This probably doesn't affect your strategy significantly as, for most startups, branding activity consists primarily of public relations (we weren't planning on buying a Super Bowl ad). This kind of brand advertising is no substitute for strong direct response marketing. For a business to grow from its early incubation to an effective company with product market fit, it must find a repeatable, scalable way to find new customers.

If press happens, great! It's nice when the world hears about our startup, but it doesn't pay the bills. My mother loves it when I get press – but you should think twice if you were thinking that your marketing dollars should be spent on press when you could spend that money on things that directly bring new customers. Press won't make your company great. We spend money to build a business. So the pedagogy of this book is this: Lean Startups use direct response tactics to align sales and marketing activity with the on-going experimentation of their business model testing.

Paying For Results

There is a process to acquiring a customer. For many products it is pretty similar: They hear about you somehow, they do a Google search for a related product, they look at your web site, they click around, they look at your pricing page, they Google for a discount code, they eventually purchase.

Regardless of whether your process is like this or different, there is a process and that process can be broken down to its discrete component parts. Every step in the process can be defined, and measured. A method for valuing advertising mechanisms in general is critical to understanding the effectiveness of each individual mechanism.

The starting point for marketing measurement is valuing the general probability of a visitor converting when they arrive at your site. That is to say, the first number you need is "On average, 1% of all visitors to our site become customers." If you don't know that number yet, then that is what you work on first. How can you test if you don't know where you start? Even if you don't know the value of customer, let's start by measuring customer acquisition. That is the first question you should be able to answer. And one of your most important goals is to make that number go up. Why is this the most important number? The connection to revenue is direct and tangible. If we ran a smoothie shop and 1% of the people who walked by in the mall bought a smoothie, if everything else remained constant and we increased that number to 1.5% then revenue increased 50%!

From there, it is broken down by lead source ("where the traffic comes from"). This is about valuing traffic. Some sources of traffic have high conversion rates because the alignment between their visitors and people that want your product are high. Some traffic sources have low conversion rates because the alignment is low or the advertising mechanism works poorly. Regardless, measuring the different in conversion rates between traffic sources is the key to understanding the differences in relative value of comparable inventory. Inventory is what publishers call locations on their site that you can buy for showing advertisements. Publishers call it "inventory" because it is what they have to sell. Each page is a perishable good.[3] If they do not sell it, it goes bad and is wasted. The result is that publishers are highly motivated to sell their inventory.

By establishing a value for each place you advertise, you can determine where your most effective advertising placements are and extend those. Even in thinking about search engine results pages ("SERPs") such as Google search results, one can conceptualize a keyword or term as a piece of inventory (i.e. a thing you can buy) having a value. The term represents inventory; the SERP pages created by people searching on those terms. We express the value created by inventory (and other mechanisms) in terms of their cost per action or CPA.

---

3. Hence, pages on the Internet and bananas have much in common.

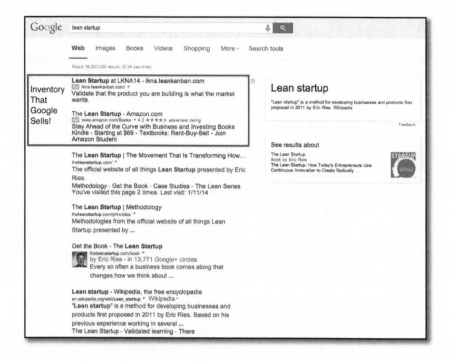

The action could be anything: A purchase, a registration for a newsletter, a subscription, an app download. The important thing is that it should be tied to something with financial value. If you know the value of an action and the cost per action, you can determine the marginal profit. So a given piece of inventory has a certain likelihood of a person engaging with an ad you show, visiting your product, and making a purchase. Given a price for that inventory, a CPA can be calculated by determining the amount that must be spent on that inventory to generate an action. Every piece of inventory, over a sufficiently long horizon, has some positive value.

Let's walk through assessing the value in an example of buying display banners on a per impression basis, then we will do a similar example looking at Google and discuss how we conceptualize the problem in the context of search terms. With these two examples, we will have a starting point for how we think about measuring value in marketing and advertising.

CPM is "cost per mille" (Greek for thousands). This is how newspapers, radio, TV and many digital advertisers have historically sold their inventory of ads. So a CPM is the price you pay to buy 1,000 views. If I buy 100,000 ad banner impressions on ESPN that costs $8 per CPM and those 100,000 impressions turn into 100 clicks, which then turn into 1 purchase of $100, then it cost me $80 to generate $1 worth of revenue. The cost per action was $800 and the average value of an action was $100. The click-through rate was 0.1% and the conversion rate was 1% (the percent of site visitors that turned into buyers.

Go back and re-read that again. There was a lot of math there, but it is self explanatory if you take it slow.

Similarly, you may have a keyword on Google that generates a steady stream of clicks for $0.75 and every 100 clicks, two people make a $100 purchase. This keyword has a different conversion rate: 2%. Visitors to the site based on that keyword are more likely to convert than visitors in the preceding example. So for this term, it costs $75.00 to generate $200.00 in revenue.

	Imps	Clicks	Convs	Click-though Rate (CTR)	Conversion Rate (CVR)	Cost	Cost per Action (CPA)
ESPN		100	2		2%	$150	$75
Google	100,000	100	1	0.1%	1%	$800	$800

Clearly, one of these is a terrible purchase and one may be pretty good (depending on your economics). This same kind of logic can be applied at almost every level of marketing and driving traffic around your site. You could use this to test creatives ("creatives" being the industry term for the banner ad). (If you found a creative that generated 10% click-through rates with the same conversion rate, the ESPN buy would be great!) Different creatives, even on the same site, will perform differently and attract different kinds of customers. You will find marketing in this way consists of hundreds of tests. As these tests lead you to new conclusions, the metrics that interest you and the tests you perform to understand and optimize your work will correspondingly change. But your interest in this high level snapshot will be eternal.

As you test marketing techniques and their efficacy, each technique or term can be thought of as having a volume and a backend conversion price. For example, there are only so many impressions you can buy on ESPN. Or there are only so many searches for "t-shirts with a koala" on Google. So for any given "thing you could buy" for marketing from a direct response perspective, there is a limit to the amount of that thing that you can purchase.

So if you have found that this "t-shirt with a koala" term generates $10 in revenue for every $5 you spend, that does not mean that you have a magic money machine that endlessly prints an infinite amount of money. The amount of money you can generate is constrained by the quantity of traffic you can buy at that price. We could express that with a graph.

In the context of Google, there are a variety of mechanisms you can manipulate to try to generate more volume. Google's favorite mechanism is to recommend that you increase your bid. It could be that at $5 you are only winning a limited amount of auctions. In the graph above, the relationship between the price paid to acquire a given customer and the number of customers is linear – as the price increases, the number of acquirable customers increases. This curve could come in a variety of shapes.

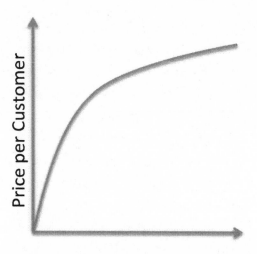

In this example, price sharply spikes before customer acquisition accelerates, but after that spike, minimal price increases will drive significant incremental customer acquisition. But this model does not accurately capture what the aggregation of customer demand probably looks like.

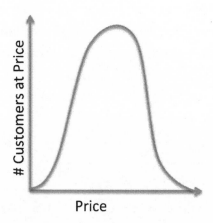

This graph represents a very effective way to think about the problem. Here, the number of total customers you have acquired is represented by the volume under the curve. As you can see, at very low prices, you can acquire very few customers. At some "sweet spot" of prices, you acquire much of your volume, then at some maximum, no matter how much you spend on marketing, you cannot acquire another customer. So each technique/price point can be plotted on this curve. You may have a system to acquire 5 customers for $2 each, another system with a maximum volume that allows you to acquire 10 more customers paying $2.50 each. And so on, and so on.

While there is some outer limit to the number of customers you can acquire (for example, the number of people on earth is a constraint), a more realistic limit not represented in this graph is the marginal profitability of the product. If we are selling super widgets for $99 and it costs us $69.00 to manufacture one, then it stands to reason that regardless of the shape of the curve, the most I am willing to spend to acquire customers would be $30.00.[4] (Or maybe $29.99 represents some desire to be profitable.)

It is not unreasonable to assume that from the perspective of marketing these prices are fixed. So the biggest sources of leverage in the model are when things are improved that impact the value of all traffic. If an optimization of the conversion path makes traffic to the site twice as likely to convert as previously, suddenly the amount of value extracted from each marketing channel has doubled.

Assuming a customer only buys one, then the Lifetime Customer Value (LCV) is $30.00. That means that customer acquisition costs, to generate incremental profit, must be less than $30.00.

---

4. Things like volume discounts and efficiency can easily be inserted into this model.

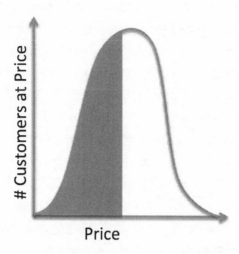

Here you can see how the marginal profit of the company constrains the amount of customer that the company can acquire. Increasing marginal revenue and profit allows the company to acquire more customers. The value of customers to the business is expressed in the form of their Lifetime Customer Value.

University of Mybills

$$LCV = \frac{ARPU}{\#months} \times Gross\ Margins \times \frac{Avg.\ Lifespan\ of}{Customers\ (in\ months)}$$

Every business has a Lifetime Customer Value and in the world of direct response, it is the alpha and the omega. For a Software as a Service (SaaS) business, or any business with recurring fees, the LCV (sometimes called the LVC or Lifetime Value of a Customer) is the product of average revenue per user (sometimes called ARPU) per month, the gross margin, and the average lifespan of customers (expressed in months) Many businesses have a different view of how LCV is calculated for their industry, but it all ends up the same: A single number that describes the value of customers. You need to know this number for your business.

The customer acquisition payback period and LCV is a gauge for how aggressive a company can be marketing and selling its services. The longer the payback period, the greater the risk that a customer churns and the marketing dollars paid to acquire the customer are lost, and vice versa. The most efficient businesses recover the cost of acquiring a customer in 6 months. Generally speaking, if the customer acquisition cost ("CAC") is over 12 months, the business is challenged.

For businesses with recurring revenue, the LCV is the net present value (NPV) of future revenue streams incorporating churn rates. So such a business may say they charge $5.00 per month (with $2 cost of good sold (COGS)) and the average customer remains for 15 months. Not taking into account a discount rate, they may say they have a $45 LCV (($5-$2)*15).

Similarly, an advertising business (like a content-based publishing site) might realize that the average consumer views 6 pages per visit, visits 5 times per month and stays a consistent visitor for 3 months. If they generate $3.00 RPMs (revenue per thousand page views, as opposed to the CPM, which we discussed earlier - the CPM being what the advertiser pays to access that inventory, resulting in revenue for the publisher), they might say that the value of a new visitor to their site would be approximately $0.27. (6 x 5 x 3 x (3/1000))[5]

---

5. I would add an exclamation mark, but I don't want to make it a factorial!!!

The payback period is important because as you make changes that you believe change retention long term, it can take a substantial amount of time to see the effect. If you make a change that causes the average new customer to stay three months longer, you may not be able to measure the change for a year or more. The shorter the period to payback, the more aggressive you can be about investing to make changes.

In a frictionless world, if LCV is greater than $0, you have a business. In the real world, the LCV needs to be a fair bit bigger. More specifically, the LCV needs to be bigger than the cost to acquire a user. If you think about this model or the recurring revenue model, you can see the many different ways in which LCV can be manipulated. All of these can be improved with aggressive testing:

1. You could charge more or get customers to buy more stuff.
2. You could drive down COGS.
3. You could get customers to stay for a longer period of time (buying more products or paying monthly or annual fees decreasing churn).

All of this speaks to the value of creating an impactful business. Effective marketing starts with maximizing the opportunity for marketing to be effective. This means giving yourself the most marginal profit per marketing dollar spent and the largest direct budget to acquire customers.

You can look at more mature markets to understand the power of being good at this. Consider the online mortgage lead market. Companies such as LowerMyBills essentially made a business of finding leads for mortgage brokers. The essence of their business model was having more brokers to sell each lead to because each broker was willing to pay between $5 and $10 for a lead. If they had a mortgage lead and sold it to five brokers for $5 per broker, they made $25. If they sold it to 10 brokers, they made $50. If they had 100 brokers, they could make $500. LowerMyBills successfully managed to draw ahead in signing up mortgage brokers and suddenly a customer was worth $20 to $50 more to them than to any other mortgage broker because LowerMyBills was so good at monetizing them. Once this happened, LowerMyBills experienced a network effect: They were willing to pay more for leads in every marketing channel than anyone else was. The result was they got all the leads. As they amassed more leads, more mortgage brokers signed up with them to buy leads. This pushed them even farther ahead in the monetization race. Being better at turning customers into money made them better at direct response marketing than their competitors. TNS Media indicated in 2006 that LowerMyBills was one of the largest advertisers in the entire Internet. When they were acquired by Experian for more than $330 million dollars, they had $26 million in profits on $120 million in sales.[1]

The University of Phoenix, a for-profit school, is no different. Their business is selling enrollment in classes they offer. There are many, many online universities, but the one that is top of mind to everyone is the University of Phoenix. This is because they did an outstanding job of optimizing their conversion process. They refined their process to such a degree that they were able to turn an email address on a landing page into someone signed up for classes so efficiently that just getting the email address of an interested consumer was worth several dollars to them. Think about what they did there: By only needing an email to start a customer down the path, they simplified the conversion. If you were a traffic-driving partner of online universities and had to choose between collecting email addresses and signing up people for classes online, you chose email addresses every time. For the traffic driving partner, it felt like a sure thing. For the University of Phoenix, with their optimized conversion process, turning email addresses into class registrations was a sure thing. With this simple conversion process, conversion rates skyrocketed compared to other online university experiences. If their conversion rate doubled, they could pay twice as much for traffic and get the same cost per lead. On the other end, when they got your email address, they had excellent sales people that closed consumers. In the same fashion as LowerMyBills, once Phoenix got a little bit ahead here, they were positioned for success. Ad Networks forced to choose which universities' ad they would show inevitably chose Phoenix because it paid better. Suddenly Phoenix had all the education leads. Then they had all the money.

At its peak, the University of Phoenix had more than 600,000 students enrolled and spent more than $300 million annually on digital marketing.[2]

To build your scalable growth engine, you need to figure out how to build an exceptional LCV for your customers. The more valuable a customer is to you, the more you can erect market barriers and the more of the market you can capture. Always have a plan to increase LCV.

Here is a slide from Mint.com's original business plan. The way they thought about revenue was the conversion rate and CPA for various products they could sell their customers.

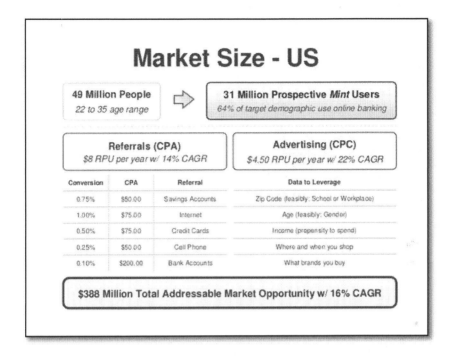

Investors were buoyed by the variety of products and flexibility of this business model. If they were able to demonstrate to a bank that they could generate new bank accounts for them, these CPAs were more like the floor than the average. Did you want to be the bank losing Mint customer accounts, or the bank gaining them. They follow that slide up with a slide on the value creation.

Value to Partners

Prospective Partner	Product or Service	Customer Acquisition Cost[1]	Mint Referral	Value Proposition
Wamu	Savings Accounts	$200.00	$50.00	$150.00
Comcast	Internet	$200.00	$75.00	$125.00
Capital One	Credit Cards	$150.00	$75.00	$75.00
Cingular	Cell Phone	$325.00	$50.00	$275.00
Wells Fargo	Bank Accounts	$175.00	$125.00	$50.00
E-Trade	Brokerage Accounts	$475.00	$100.00	$375.00
Blue Cross	Insurance	$225.00	$100.00	$125.00
Bank of America	Mortgage	$550.00	$325.00	$225.00

Partners can increase revenue via cost-effect customer acquisition

If you go find that deck online, you will see that these are the slides that sold investors. Pre-product, all Mint.com had going for it was a very clear plan to have extraordinary LCV. You should have the same vision for how you will create value. And have a plan to increase it.

Having said that, you should not allow all of your tests and transactions to be simplified down into just an LCV. Typically, revenue distribution by customer doesn't follow a normal distribution because the amounts are not regular.

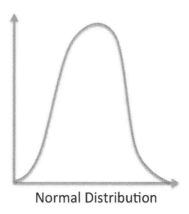

Normal Distribution

We aren't talking about the average weight of a person, we are talking about how much money customers give you.[3] This varies widely! A more common result of plotting revenue per customer is a power law distribution.

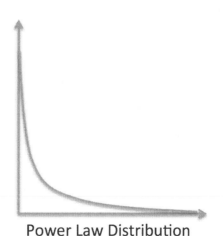

Power Law Distribution

In a power law distribution, there are a few cust~
much more than others. This can result in ske
For example, if an A/B test signs up one cust

matically more than everyone else, it could pull up the average for that result.

It is likely in the early going of a business that your understanding of the revenue distribution of your business will be incomplete due to lack of customers, but one other tension that can prevent the power law from appearing is problems with pricing models. An overly simplistic model that does not change pricing as value to customers changes can prevent the power law from appearing when you plot it. But the goal is for this kind of understanding to emerge. Don't let one large new customer change what you think the expected LCV of any random new customer will be.

Regardless, an understanding of profit in various outcomes is important and while an LCV may simplify the profitability analysis of your business, it is important to have benchmarks to inform aspects of your business such as marketing spend, while never completely reducing your understanding of your business to these numbers. Embrace complexity!

Notes

1. http://en.wikipedia.org/wiki/LowerMyBills.com
2. http://en.wikipedia.org/wiki/University_of_Phoenix
3. http://data.heapanalytics.com/your-average-revenue-per-customer-is-meaningless/

CHAPTER 3

The Marketing Funnel

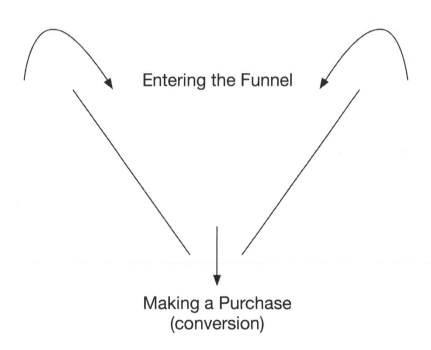

Entering the Funnel

Making a Purchase
(conversion)

M arketers typically think of their job similar to sales in that there is a funnel that prospects must be driven through to be acquired and converted to customers. At the top of the funnel are prospects "entering" the funnel. They are becoming aware that the product exists or maybe even simply becoming aware that they have a problem. From awareness of the problem, they become aware that there are solutions to the problem. "I am thirsty."; "When people drink things, they are not thirsty any more. I could drink something!" From here, depending on the nature of the product, a marketer will attempt to establish the merits of their product and then enable a sale of the product. "North Pole Water quenches thirst like no other drink could ever possibly quench one's thirst."; "North Pole Water is available very close to me at a price that is comparable to other thirst quenching options."; "If I click this button, a cool, refreshing glass of North Pole Water will magically materialize in front of me."

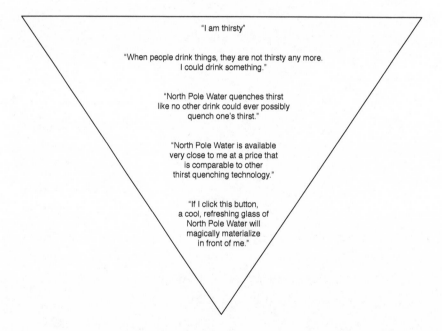

Why a funnel? Because for every prospect that enters at the top, only a fraction of customers emerge from the bottom. Sometimes customers don't find the pain significant enough to purchase any product ("I'm not that thirsty."), sometimes they choose a competitor.

The nature of this funnel varies as product purchase sophistication varies from impulse purchases to complex purchase decisions. For example, a pack of bubble gum is typically thought of as an impulse purchase. You always see a pack of bubble gum available at the checkout counter at your grocery store because very, very few people go to the grocery store thinking, "I need a pack of bubble gum," then wander the store looking for gum. But many, many people, while standing in the checkout counter line, see a pack of gum and think "Yum, maybe I should buy that pack of gum." The nature of that sales funnel is very different than a car dealership. Very few people drive by a car lot and think, "I will buy a car today." Gum is an impulse purchase - the thing most easily sold in a moment's time in a grocery store. A car is a considered purchase. There is typically research a consumer does before making a decision and helping the consumer more easily do this research (and swaying the results!) is a large part of how marketers think about considered purchase problems.

When marketers think about their funnel, they will want to invest in a continuum of marketing activities at a variety of points along the funnel. Most have a ratio in their heads of prospects to final customers and how those ratios work at various points along the funnel. Ten percent of customers that become thirsty will buy North Pole Water because 30% will choose not to quench their thirst and 60% will choose competing products. For North Pole Water marketing to work (i.e. The business meets its revenue goals), they need to make sure that a certain amount of people become aware of their thirst, that a certain amount of people decide to quench it, and that a certain amount of people choose their product over competitors. The manner in which you might do that marketing may differ from place to place in the funnel and this needs to be accounted for in the marketing plan.

Typically, bottom of the funnel activities have the highest ROI and are the easiest to justify. These are people that are thirsty and love North Pole Water already. We just need to push them over the hump: "North Pole Water is sold ten feet from you at low, low prices!" This marketing typically converts well. If you are reaching those very, very specific audiences with a North Pole marketing message, it results in a sale. If you are just trying to make people aware that North Pole Water exists (consideration, as it is called by marketers), or to prefer North Pole Water to competitors (preference, as it is known), that is a critical activity – you do not want to constrain marketing to people that already love you – but it typically has lower returns. That is, people that are trying to decide what to buy are less likely to choose you than people that are trying to buy your product.

Internet advertising plays a large role in every aspect of the funnel. In 2011, Internet advertising revenues in the United States surpassed those of cable television and nearly exceeded those of broadcast television.

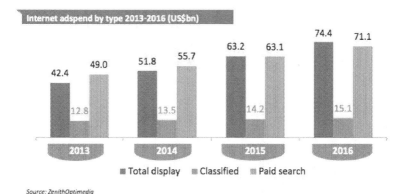

Source: ZenithOptimedia

Zenith Optimedia reports that Internet advertising will make up more than 23% of total advertising spend in 2014 and that will continue to grow with 16% annual growth in Internet advertising spend each year through 2016[1]. Maybe the most amazing thing about this huge market is that it did not exist 20 years ago.

Notes

1. http://techcrunch.com/2014/04/07/internet-ad-spend-to-reach-121b-in-2014-23-of-537b-total-ad-spend-ad-tech-gives-display-a-boost-over-search/

CHAPTER 4

The History of Digital Data

1995: A VISION FOR DIGITAL ADVERTISING

W hen you attempt to visit a web site from your computer, your computer reaches across the Internet to the server where the website is hosted and makes a request for that page on that web site. That request may consist of images, HTML pages, CSS (formatting), javascript (interactive elements), or any of a range of content types and other assets that contribute to the page to make it what it is. Each time you request a page, the server is aware that you requested this page because you requested it from the server. This gives that server the opportunity to note that such a request has been made.

Each website server contains a log file which enumerates every request for a file on that site. This includes every graphical file and every web page. This means that when we discuss website traffic, we are able to have a unique record in the logs of every single request made for every single page or portion of a page on a website.

```
127.0.0.1 - the_user_name [31/Dec/2013:23:59:59
-0700] "GET /image.gif HTTP/1.0" 200 2428
"http://www.example.com/index.html" "Safa-
ri/531.21.10"
```

Standard log file entry with IP address, logged in user name, timestamp, file requested, status code, file size, referrer, and user agent

In many ways, the vision for digital advertising came from technologists. Technologists looked at digital advertising starting with websites. To understand how they thought about the opportunity for advertising, you must understand a little about websites. This is foundational because how a site works is a microcosm of how everything on the Internet works. A site and the things that happen on it is a convenient and well-understood metaphor for every transaction on the Internet.

At the advent of website development, marketers realized that website analytics could give them something they had never had before in the history of advertising: a real-time dashboard of how consumers interacted with their marketing content. Marketers built web sites and accompanying simple analytic tools to help understand them. But just because you built it did not mean that they would come. To the extent that the website represented an effective marketing tool, it was important to drive traffic to it in much the same way that retailers or restaurants attempt to drive foot traffic into their stores. Without traffic, justifying the marketing expenditure of web site development would be difficult or impossible.

Companies like Wired sold the first ads in 1996 and several large advertisers were eager to partner with Wired and experiment with the first organized effort to drive traffic to other sites via advertising. Technology and technologists were able to support this activity using the same underlying technology. By hosting the image files that represented the banner advertisements on the same or similar servers as the web site, log files were created in exactly the same fashion. This allowed technology to demonstrate exactly how many people viewed the banner. One simply counted the number of times the image that represented the banner was requested. Quickly, the technologists were able to make just a few enhancements to track the user as a user went from a banner to the website itself. Now advertisers showing the same banners in different locations could count the observations of that banner in each place.

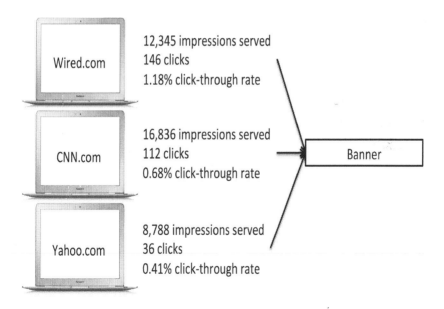

In this fashion, marketers were able to build a model where they could see both where banners were being displayed and where banners were being clicked. Never before had an advertiser had a tool that allowed them to say - in real-time - "When I showed this ad in this place, at this time, consumers were more likely to interact with it, engage with it, and relate to my brand message". Unparalleled insight into advertising efficacy.

Performance Advertising

If this had been digital advertising's only contribution to the advertising industry, it would have been significant. However the change digital advertising wrought did not end there. Soon marketers realized that with the power of this technology it was possible to create a new marketplace for advertising that recognized the value of performance.

Previously, the impact of advertising felt ephemeral - John Wanamaker thought half of it was wasted! There was no way to tell exactly how many people looked at an advertisement in a newspaper. There was no way to tell exactly how many people saw an advertisement on television. Both industries invested heavily in technologies to better estimate the value of their marketing contribution, but systems such as Nielsen used panels to approximate viewership. "We looked at the TV shows that 1,000 people approximating all Americans watched last night and have determined that 3.2 million people watched your ad last night!" The Internet offered the ability to determine precisely how many people had been exposed to an advertising message.

With the new technology of Internet advertising, marketers found a new and unique opportunity for direct attribution of advertising. To the extent it was now possible to measure precisely the number of clicks a specific piece of advertising inventory facilitated for an advertiser, shouldn't it be possible for an advertiser to pay only for advertising that drove traffic to the advertiser's website?

This concept triggered a revolution in advertising. Now the direct value of a page on the Internet could be imputed from its ability to drive traffic to advertisers website.

The first company to take advantage of this was Google. In all the ways that matter, Google search results pages are simply another example of inventory, or pages available to be advertised on by advertisers. The search result pages are generally viewed as the most valued pages to advertisers on the Internet. Consider this: if someone searches for high definition television, they are likely in the market for a high definition television. Advertisers found that showing ads for high definition televisions on Google search result pages where users were searching for high-definition televisions was an extraordinarily effective tool for advertising. Those people clicked on the ads and bought high definition televisions. Click-through rates were high, conversion rates were high, CPAs were low.

Even today there is no finer mechanism for reaching in-market customers than search results pages. Google built one of the most valuable companies on earth using the basic premise of our book: the ability to associate a page with its value to an advertiser defines the value of that page.

Evolution of Online Advertising: Google as 800lb Gorilla of Digital Advertising

Google was not the first to sell advertising online, but their strategic decision to offer advertising on search result pages and be paid only when a consumer clicked on an advertisement on those pages has fundamentally reshaped the way people think about digital advertising. Today advertisers spend billions of dollars attempting to better optimize their opportunity to bid on Google search result pages. Amazingly their optimizations are so effective that the dollars saved from optimization are generally reinvested in further Google advertising.

The Internet bubble of 2000 can be attributed to a lack of monetization, among other things. Old people such as myself recollect the bubble as a time of dot.coms "acquiring eyeballs" and people spent millions and millions of dollars acquiring eyeballs, but there was no way to convert those eyeballs into dollars. Google's AdSense network completely change that. Released in 2003, AdSense created a platform for almost any publisher to monetize content. Suddenly eyeballs had demonstrable value.

On the other side of the marketplace, advertisers found the ability to advertise on Google incredibly compelling in two respects: First, advertisers could see their ad the moment they placed it in Google's search advertising platform. If they purchased the word "TV" and bid high enough, (and in 2003, one did not have to bid very high) they could instantly see their ad on the "TV" search result page; a powerful demonstration to the advertiser of the effectiveness of their advertising. Second, the advertisers knew they were only paying for clicks. They never needed to worry that, for example, when they search for TV and saw their ad, they would have to pay for that. That "test view" was a free taste for the advertiser of the power of advertising with Google, particularly for small businesses.

Individual publishers existed as well, and each of them attempted to sell their digital advertising space. However the space was typically sold on a CPM basis. Here, advertisers paid for the display of their ad rather than paying for any more sophisticated performance - a much lower perceived value. Why was every publisher not able to implement Google's performance-based pricing? Mostly, it is terrifying for a publisher that has always sold things one way to sell things a different way. But I am sure they would say there are other reasons: first, they simply did not have as much inventory as Google did. Google today is one of the most popular sites on the Internet generating billions of page views per day. When Google got started, any money was good money. They had no revenue expectation. Other publishers frequently view their digital product as replacing other revenue. Second, Google's advertising was incredibly effective. Most publishers simply did not have enough inventory that performed well enough to be able to sell advertising using that model. People searching for "TV" were highly likely to click an ad for TV. People reading the news were far less likely to click that same ad. This meant that the amount made per page was much, much higher for Google's relevant content. This touches one of our core theses: People on Google are lower in the funnel - when they start searching for something, that is when an ad for it is most likely to be effective. Other publishers, reaching consumers at higher points in the funnel, were doomed to be selling less effective advertising.

Finally, Google had advertising scale. Google has millions of businesses, many of them very small, that collectively bid up the value of Google's inventory. With so many bidders, almost every query has a reasonable effective CPM for Google. The average publisher saddled with small-scale and frequently poor performing inventory could not afford to build their business in the same fashion that Google has today.

One last easily understood reason is that these businesses were grounded in nondigital business models. Many of the Internet's early publishers experience with monetizing content came from other media forms. In print or TV or radio, CPM sales models are the rule. Without the power of digital attribution, eyeballs are the order of the day.

Google's 100% investment in digital combined with rapid growth and incredible scale allowed it to offer a new model, reliant on digital technology, that used the power of attribution and demonstrated value to reshape the advertising equation for almost every advertiser. It demonstrated the compelling power of native advertising in the search format and made Google the largest media company in the world.

CHAPTER 5

But How Does This Work?

HTML

It is great to know that we want to track all the people that click through from Google and elsewhere and see how many conversions they generate and the value of those conversions, but it is something else to do it. We need to instrument our product to provide us with rich feedback about how users experience it. To really understand the best practices here and what we need to do, we need to understand how this works and dig into the technology.

Once you know how the core aspects of Internet technology work, we can relate back complex aspects of Internet advertising to these simple core themes. In a single chapter, I will turn you into someone that knows how these systems work from the very base of the tech stack: The code, the algorithms, the whole nine yards.

The starting point is you and your browser.

Let's walk through a browser making a request for a page (and associated ads). When you click a link or open a page, your browser makes a "request" for content. That request receives a "response" from a web server. I want to talk about the request, but I think the easiest way to ramp up is to talk about the response first. The response to a request for a web page is HTML. HTML is Hypertext Markup Language - the language of web pages. Hypertext was the original name for what you saw on a web page. "Hyper" comes from the Greek word meaning "beyond", so the idea was that text with links in it was "Beyond Text"!

In 1993, HTML was so easy that even I knew everything there was to know about it.

```
<HTML>Hello World</HTML>
```

Boom, I made an HTML page. The text in brackets is my Hypertext Markup, making this HTML. The <HTML> denotes the beginning of a Hypertext Markup document. The </HTML> denotes the end. There are many other elements of HTML that are easily understood. In fact, much of the success of the web is because this is the case:

```
<HTML>
<B>Hello World</B>
</HTML>
```

Hello World

I made it bold!

```
<HTML>
<IMG
SRC="http://google.com/picture_of_a_horse.gif">
<B>Hello World</B>
</HTML>
```

Now I have pre-pended the text with an image ("img" - HTML is case insensitive) of a cat, the source file ("SRC") for that picture being hosted on google.com and the file itself named "picture_of_a_horse.gif". The HTTP stands for "Hypertext Transfer Protocol", the "kind" of request that it should make to get the file.

Now I will wrap it with an anchor ("<A>") tag that links it to a hypertext reference ("HREF"). This is a terribly technical way to describe: "I am going to make it link to another page". Here I go:

```
<HTML>
<A HREF="http://google.com/">
<IMG
SRC="http://google.com/picture_of_a_cat.gif">
<B>Hello World</B>
</A>
</HTML>
```

Now if you click the image or the text "Hello World", it will link you to google.com. Hopefully, I didn't just blow your mind, but the great thing about a book is that you are welcome to stare at this page as long as you want.

Obviously, this book is not for people looking to acquire technical skills.

HTML has gotten much more complicated. There is now a programming language (javascript) that you can supplement to handle things like making elements of the page slide and move along with other programmatic aspects of the page. Also, there is a formatting language (Cascading Style Sheets or "CSS") that controls the layout of the page, making sure that text is the right color and size, the background is the right color, and generally that every pixel is where it is meant to be.

So when you click on that link requesting the google.com home page, the computer hosting google.com responds back with a document almost exactly like the one we just described. There is probably more: A request for an associated javascript or CSS file might be embedded in the page, along with a set of images, setting off a chain of requests to the server. The manner in which they are embedded is not dissimilar from the way that we embedded the picture of a cat. So the request is made for the page, the browser realizes that the page contains several other documents, be they images, javascript or other stuff, and seamlessly requests all of that content as well before laying out the page for your enjoyment.

IFrames

One specific thing that we can dwell on for a moment because it is a recurring theme is an iframe. This is another example of a way to request a document that is associated with the page. An iframe is an embedded frame in a page. It looks like this in an HTML document:

```
<Iframe    src="http://google.com"    width=300
height=100></iframe>
```

It works very similar to a picture or text, but in this example, it creates a 300 pixel wide and 100 pixel high space on the page and proceeds to load the contents of the Google homepage into that space.

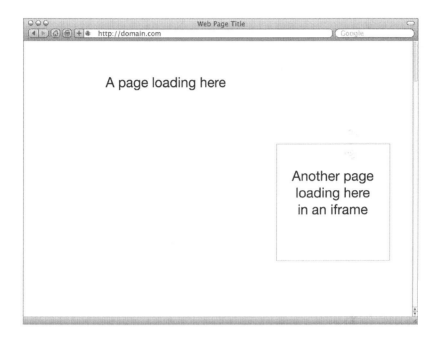

Iframes are very common in advertising because they allow an advertisement to be requested and loaded asynchronously from the rest of the page. As the page begins to layout, it can look at this iframe and create that 300x100 window and then move on to laying out the rest of the page. If google.com was down and the frame never loads any content, it is of no consequence to the rest of the page. Publishers love this because it means that they don't need to wait for an advertiser to send them an ad to display before moving on to the rest of the page. They can put the ad in an iframe on the page! The page can render and display basically correctly, while waiting for the response to the iframe request.

In our prior example, when rendering the page with the cat image, the page layout must wait until the image response is received before the rest of the page can be displayed because it is not obvious what the dimensions of the image are prior to downloading the image itself. Hence the page will "hang" while waiting for the image to download so the browser can determine how to format the page.

Iframes are useful for improving the consumer experience as a publisher because you don't want an advertisers slow response to hold your content captive.

Many of the pages you look at on the Internet every day have one or more iframes in them.

HTTP Requests

Now that you have a vivid understanding of how web servers respond with content, we can talk about how the request works. So when a browser goes to request a resource (an image, page or whatever) using HTTP, it connects to the server that hosts the resource it is seeking (for example www.brenthalliburton.com is a web server that hosts my site) and sends a message requesting the file. The request looks a lot like this:

```
GET /path/file.html HTTP/1.0
[blank line here]
```

That's it. You have a request to the server to "GET" the document on the web server in the "path" folder named "file.html" using the HTTP 1.0 protocol.

Many browsers add a few things to the request in the form of other headers. An example might be a user-agent header that identifies the kind of browser:

```
GET /path/file.html HTTP/1.0
User-Agent: BestBrowserEver/1.0
[blank line here]
```

So someone is using BestBrowserEver (as opposed to Chrome or Internet Explorer or Safari) to request the page. The server might use this information to customize the page slightly to better serve the user. There are literally dozens of headers that might be passed by a browser depending on the kind of request, browser, and site.

Another great header is the "If-Modified-Since" header. It typically looks like this:

```
If-Modified-Since:   Fri, 31 Dec 1999 23:59:59
GMT
```

This allows a browser to request a resource from a server, but tells the server that the resource only needs to be sent if it has not changed since it last checked. This saves bandwidth and can accelerate page load times. Thus a smartly designed web site will structure content that re-occurs on every or many pages throughout a web site such as images, css and javascript into an external file pulled in by each page. Then when that file is pulled into the content for the first time, it can set the header and it will not need to be pulled in again.

I know this is pretty down in the weeds, but bear with me. This will all be relevant and useful to you. Let's talk about how the server responds and then we will turn this into business. This is the level of geekiness you need to know to be awesome.

So I told you before that the server responds with the HTML document. This was a sin of omission. Before it responds with the document, it responds with an HTTP status code. That might look like this:

```
HTTP/1.1 200 OK
Date: Fri, 31 Dec 2012 23:59:59 GMT
Content-Type: text/html
Content-Length: 23
some-footer: some-value
another-footer: another-value

<HTML>Hello World</HTML>
```

So here we sent an HTTP status response of 200 – an "OK" message. A 200 code means "no problem, here comes the document". So now we tell them the type of document (An HTML document), we tell them how long the document is (23 characters), maybe we pass some footers (similar to the HTTP headers), and then we send the document.

That isn't particularly interesting, but what is germane to our discussion is the 301 status code. A 200 HTTP status response is what is sent when the document is returned. A 301 does something else:

```
HTTP/1.1 301 Moved Permanently
Location: http://www.brenthalliburton.com/
```

This response means that the request made should be redirected to a new location. (In this case, the new location is http://www.brenthalliburton.com/) The 3XX class of status codes provides an invaluable tool for online advertisers because it means that a request made to one location can be passed around to many servers. Soon we will learn exactly how useful that is.

How Cookies Work

We have gotten pretty technical, but there are things that we haven't mentioned yet. It's time we talk about the elephant in the room: Cookies! If a consumer knows anything about online advertising besides how annoying it is, it is that cookies are something that sound pleasant but may be nefarious!

Cookies are the last piece of technology we need to know about to understand measurement and attribution in the digital space.

First, what is a cookie? A cookie is a small piece of data sent from a site and stored in a user's web browser while a user is browsing that web site. When the user browses the same web site in the future, the data stored in the cookie is sent back to the website by the browser. Cookies were designed to be a reliable mechanism for websites to remember the state of the website or activity the user had taken in the past.

The web as you know it would not exist without cookies. Let me give you an example or two of the amazing things that cookies do unrelated to online advertising. First, your shopping cart works because of cookies. When you click "I want to buy that book" on Amazon, it sets a cookie that uniquely identifies you on your browser, and makes an entry in its database that this identifier selected this book. Then when you go to your checkout page, it receives your unique identifier from your browser and displays the appropriate books you previously selected. Without cookies, after you added a book to your shopping cart, Amazon would have no way to connect the shopping cart to you.

Second, when you login to a web site like Gmail, cookies are what allow them to remember who you are as you look at your inbox. When you check the "remember me" box, it sets a "persistent cookie" that can last for a long period of time, so each time you come back to Gmail, it sees that this ID has returned and displays the appropriate inbox.

The World Wide Web is what engineers call "stateless". Each request from a browser is completely independent of any other request. While there are many benefits to this, the ability of cookies to introduce maintaining state and allowing information about a user to persist from request to request is extraordinarily valuable.

We've already turned you into a giant web geek, so we might as well talk about the technology underlying cookies for a moment. Imagine a straightforward GET request – this is how most web pages on the Internet are requested. A browser "GET"s a page from the server:

```
GET /index.html HTTP/1.1
Host: www.cogmap.com
```

Now the response header that comes back looks something like this:

```
HTTP/1.1 200 OK
Content-type: text/html
Set-Cookie: color=green
```

Set-Cookie is the header the server sends to the browser to (surprise!) set a cookie. Set-Cookie is a directive for the browser to store the cookie and send it back in future requests to the server if the browser supports cookies and cookies are enabled. So the next request for a page would look like this:

```
GET /blog/index.html HTTP/1.1
Host: www.cogmap.com
Cookie: color=green
```

Because the cookie was set on the preceding request, each subsequent request to the client contains the cookie value. In this way, the server knows that this request was related to the previous request.

A cookie can have both a domain and a path. These define the scope of the cookie. In the preceding example, the server domain (www.cogmap.com) is automatically used to define the scope of the cookie. This means that the cookie will only be sent by the browser when it is making a request to that particular hostname. If the user visits another site, that cookie value will never be passed.

This is a very effective tool for the modern Internet because it is owned by the user and maintains privacy. Because other sites cannot access a given sites cookie pool, no information is shared between sites. Further, because the cookies are stored in the users browsers, cookies can easily be deleted or disabled.

This is also an effective tool for advertising. If I cookie a user with a unique ID when they request a pixel from me, I could use a pixel to drop a cookie when I show them an ad and then use another pixel on the advertisers site to retrieve the cookie. If I put that second pixel on the "Thank You" page of a commerce site, for example, I could use it to demonstrate that someone I showed an ad to 3 hours ago just made a purchase by getting to the "Thank You" page.

By using pixels and cookies, I have created a closed loop attribution engine.

Data Leakage

As we talk about advertising strategies, many people will throw around aspects of third-party cookies and how they enable various advertising strategies.

While cookies are sent only to the server setting them or a server in the same Internet domain, as we have discussed, a web page may contain images or other resources stored on servers in other domains. Cookies that are set during retrieval of these components are called third-party cookies.

This is typically the case for advertising technology and it means that advertisers frequently rely on setting third party cookies. Typically the SSP, associated ad networks and ad agencies and other parties to an ad call will all have some presence on the page but not be a first party domain. However all of them are interested in tracking the user as part of their network optimization. So they all set third party cookies.

Tools like Ghostery can be installed in a browser to show third party cookie activity. In the modern Internet, you can sometimes see 20 or more cookies set by advertising players in the LUMAScape on a sophisticated publishers site.

A common debate today among browser developers, the industry, the government and consumers is whether third party cookies should be disabled in browsers by default. When considering what we have just reviewed, it seems logical to many consumers that disabling this tracking across the Internet may seem like a reasonable thing to do - it seems like few, if any, improve the consumer experience. Unfortunately for advertisers, some of the most basic functionality such as controlling the frequency that an ad is shown to a consumer relies on cookies to track the exposure a consumer has to ads. Even the most basic desktop targeting could be severely impacted by restricting the placement of third party cookies.

Consumers are not the only ones negatively affected by these cookies. While on the one hand, publishers notionally encourage these third parties to place cookies (as it is part of how those publishers maximize the revenue they accrue from these third parties), some third parties use them in a nefarious practice frequently referred to as "data leakage". Data leakage is when networks monetize impressions based on data they receive from publishers without a publisher intending them to receive this or use it for monetization. Specifically, they use it in a fashion where the revenue generated is not shared with that publisher.

For example, if an ad network drops a cookie on a user in the process of monetizing an impression on Forbes.com, regardless of the nature of that contractual relationship, it is child's play to connect that user at some later point to the visit they made to Forbes.com. If they sold an advertiser at some later date a targeted campaign of "people who have been to Forbes.com" or even used the knowledge that they visited Forbes to optimize their ad serving in some way unless they have a mechanism to share that revenue with Forbes, they have gained from their relationship with Forbes without Forbes reaping some benefit.

CHAPTER 6

Attribution Theory & Practice

The Concept of Attribution

I t is time to apologize because I am sure you were hoping by now that I would tell you "THE ONE SECRET GROWTH HACK THAT QUINTUPLES YOUR TRAFFIC". I will tell you this, but if you don't have your measurement act together, how will you know it worked? I want the credit. That means we need to have attribution nailed.

When people talk about lean startups, what they are really talking about is experiment design. This is the essence of lean because you can't conduct an experiment without measurement. In learning the underlying technology, you already know more about how measurement works in digital than ninety-nine percent of the free world so you are prepared to begin thinking about what you want to measure and how you will design the experiment.

Measurement of digital is complex, but I believe that measurement of digital is complex because we can now gather such a tremendous volume of helpful data. Far too many startups fail because they attempt to test their product in a way that ensures it fails regardless of its merits. The primary failing of lean startups is test design in marketing and sales.

Allow me to illustrate. An entrepreneur recently told me that he was finishing his initial product development (minimum viable product, or MVP, in lean-speak) and needed a drip of traffic to begin testing some assumptions. He wanted me to tell him the best way to get 50 people per day to visit his web site so he could observe their behavior. So this is a story of someone who has spent an extraordinary amount of time building a new product, has put his heart and soul into doing something very difficult, and has invested his hopes and dreams in wanting his test to go a certain way. Then when it is time to test it, he throws caution and planning to the wind! Not only does he not tell me what he wants to test, he assumes that it doesn't matter. He assumes that any random person is the same as anyone else. That is a terrible way to test an MVP. Even if you are doing a simple consumer usability test, you want to make certain assumptions around your target market. For example, Snapchat is targeted at a demographic and its usability practices need to be consistent with the expectations for that demographic. If you tested a consumer application on my retired parents, you might think you need to make massive changes to your application for it to be simple enough for consumers to use. For the purposes of getting your MVP out in the market, a more valid audience test might be more appropriate. Conversely, if you are launching an advertising platform and had me test it, you might think that your product is "good enough to use" without having a test that gave you usable data. I am an outlier because I have played with dozens of these platforms.

This is why, even in the earliest stages of product development, effective marketing and sales is important. Reaching and engaging an appropriate audience will power the success of the business.

Reaching the wrong audience will break any test. The startup is an expert in building an MVP, but constructing a proper test of an MVP is an exercise in lean marketing, which is a different skill.

Now that you have a framework for thinking about your goals (direct response funnels) and an understanding of how different parties measure those goals using web technology (you got your nerd merit badge), we can drill down into how businesses think about digital attribution and how we can use that data. We want to measure how many clicks from Google it takes to generate a conversion. That sounds eminently reasonable, but it begs the question: "How do we do that?" We need to know the number of clicks and we need to track each of those clickers all the way through your experience to measure a conversion. What if they don't click, but they see the ad and two hours later they visit our site and convert? Should we measure that? What if it was a day? What if they clicked on an ad, didn't convert, then saw a different ad and then clicked and converted? There are an infinite number of these configurations.

There isn't a perfect answer to these questions and if there were, it would be unique and highly customized to each product being sold and each company selling it. But there are good answers and there are conventional answers and that are useful to apply here.

Let's start with measuring digital events such as commerce purchases.

Technologically, measuring the event is fairly straightforward: Using a pixel, the event can send a message signaling that it has occurred and a conversion has taken place. A tiny image or javascript placed on the thank you page fires when someone visits and records that the thank you page was reached, indicating that someone made a purchase. Given the knowledge that a conversion has occurred, how would you assign "credit" for this conversion? That credit assignment is critical to understanding the value and effectiveness of media so building a strong model is important. Most current attribution models are flawed; they are too simple and easily gamed, as they measure only the conversion event and skew metrics and incentives to bias the lower-funnel tactics. Given the variables of periodicity, sequencing, type of advertising, and degree of engagement, the complexity required to build a truly accurate "fractional" attribution model can not be overcome in a single generalized case or even in extremely specific cases in most instances.

The industry has overcome this by offering up a variety of different mechanisms.

Last Click Attribution

Last click attribution is the most common attribution model employed in digital marketing. This model is simple: Whoever drove the last click wins. If a consumer sees an ad, clicks on it, does not convert, sees an ad later, then goes back to the site and converts, the click gets it! If the consumer sees 500 banners for a product, then searches and clicks on the search ad, then the search ad gets all the credit and the banners get none.

It is safe to assume that proponents of last click attribution (there are very few remaining proponents who are not proponents solely of simplicity) hope that over time the distribution of click events award everybody evenly. Unfortunately, it is widely agreed that the last click attribution model probably overvalues "bottom of the funnel" marketing tactics such as Google search ads and retargeting.

Many advertisers might supplement this model by putting a "look back" attribution window on the conversion. For example, the agency might say that only clicks that happen within 48 hours of the conversion receive credit. With this look back window, if someone clicks the ad, then two weeks later comes back to the site and converts, then the ad would receive no credit.

View-Through

View-through attribution is a less utilized but well-known measurement technique. View-through attribution models reward the publisher for showing ads to people who later convert, regardless of whether they clicked on the ad. Usually view-through attribution is handled similarly to last click attribution in that "the last viewed impression wins".

View-through attribution makes sense in the abstract: There is certainly some benefit to people seeing ads. Most of the success of TV advertisements is "view-through" in nature. To imply that showing someone an ad is not a contributor to later conversion would fly in the face of common sense.

Unfortunately, given the ability to target individual users, view-through attribution is often abused in the digital world by publishers with many ads on the page and the ability to frequency cap their ads. By frequency capping their ads at something like 1 in 24 hours, they can attempt to ensure that everyone that visits their site has seen an ad in the last 24 hours, maximizing the opportunity for the publisher to take the credit for the campaign. For particularly active performance campaigns, they might up that to something like 1 in 3 hours. This approach is referred to in the industry as "cookie-bombing" because the objective is to be the person who sets the cookie with the most recent time stamp when the user converts. By showing the ads at a very high frequency and constantly setting cookies on users, the publisher can take credit. This ad may be very low on the page or inconveniently placed, but the objective of taking the credit for the ad exposure has been achieved.

On the one hand, it might seem like the publisher is shamelessly trying to take credit for everything they possibly can. On the other, the advertiser might be achieving their goal by getting their message out in a widespread fashion.

At the peak of its fame and name recognition, Vonage, a popular VOIP service, was doing large amounts of view-though attribution-based advertising. By rewarding performance advertisers for showing their ads constantly in a semi-performance-ish manner, everyone felt like they saw Vonage ads all the time in the digital universe.

On one particularly memorable occasion, the marketing department of Vonage turned off their view-through advertising to test other techniques. Within weeks, the CEO complained to marketing that he no longer felt like he saw Vonage ads everywhere he went on the Internet.

View-through attribution-based cookie-bombing rewards saturation. This means that if your start-up is in a situation where this kind of effect is important, using view-through attribution may be valuable. Unfortunately, typically, the current usage of view-through conversions is not a success metric customers benefit from; it is a pricing mechanism by which agencies are able to imply a correlation with performance while networks are able to use their reach to spend large budgets for popular brands. So if you attempt to negotiate a CPA-based deal with a publisher or ad network, you should probably not engage in using view-through as an attribution model.

Brand Studies

Another form of attribution that is frequently discussed is the impact on the brand independent of actual conversions. An example is that Coca-Cola might say, "Do people feel more inclined to buy Coca-Cola vs. Pepsi after they see this ad?" The dream to understand this is to test versus a control population the Coke and Pepsi sales of exposed consumers. In practice, the way this works is that Coke just asks people. This information is usually gathered through the use of brand studies. A brand study consists of a survey of people exposed and not-exposed to the advertisement to gather their view on the market and brand. Comparing this test and control group allows one to see how viewing the advertisement has changed the customers perspective on the brand.

To conduct the survey, the standard best practice is to cookie people that see the ad, then target those people with a special survey collection banner. There may be some sort of prize for participation with the most common being a lottery for a gift certificate. Like real lotteries, they can have a small prize, entice a thousand people to try and win it, and get results for far cheaper than paying for each result.

The goal of these surveys is to gather information from respondents about the image of their brand and their competitor's brands, identify important brand attributes, and other related market opportunities.

Finally, these studies could have a panel component to address the real question of purchase habits, where a group of people whose identity is known have a controlled exposure to the ad and their reaction is subsequently measured. This could reveal how different demographic and psychographic characteristics affect performance of a creative message. It could also be tied back to transactional activity of a household (potentially exploiting cross-device targeting technology), revealing how the advertising triggers a propensity to change shopping habits. This means that a true ROI metric can be drawn out from the advertising, showing exactly how many dollars were generated in revenue as a result of the advertising campaign.

comScore and Nielsen are two of the most well-known companies in this space. Other companies include Millward Brown, Quantcast or, in the mobile advertising market, Placed.

For many large consumer brands, these studies are the most important metric driving marketing measurement at the company. For example, Budweiser marketing values only two metrics: sales and brand perception. It is all about making people "like" Budweiser more.

App Installs

One more kind of digital conversion that is worth considering is the app install. With the tremendous growth of mobile, one of the new things that has changed the way people think about the world is the birth of "apps". Apps like Instagram have re-shaped how social networks are formed and the value of ubiquitous apps can be measured with a "b" – billions of dollars.

Because driving app growth is critical path for so many startups and other businesses, facilitating app installation is a powerful business for advertising. This has led to the creation of a new kind of conversion: The app install. Here, advertisers pay a fee to the publisher/network for facilitating the installation of the application on a consumer phone.

In practice, the Apple Store and Android Store are black boxes. It is either impossible or very difficult to know if someone installed an app or not inside the store. So the product offered by most conversion tracking functions works like this: A banner is displayed with a link to the app in the store. When someone clicks the banner they go to the store page that allows them to download the app. When the consumer downloads the app and starts it up, upon startup a special piece of code provided by the network is called that sends the network a signal that the user has installed the app. They then match the device identifier to the identifier of people that were served ads to confirm that the installation has taken place.

This has ballooned almost overnight to an extraordinarily large industry. Writing checks to drive app installs is easy. Further, effective app install campaigns have a network effect thanks to the way that app stores are constructed. If you drive enough installs, you work your way into the "most popular apps" lists in the stores. This causes your app installs to grow at an even more accelerated rate and this growth is an organic free growth. So theoretically, all you need is a little money to juice the engine and then your app will reach terminal velocity and grow organically in a massive wave.

As you can imagine, demand for this is extremely high both among venture-funded companies that need the growth to validate the business model and regular businesses that simply need customers.

There are several kinds of businesses worth noting in this space. The first kind are what we will call "black hat" for the purpose of this discussion. There are networks that will, for a set fee, get your app on the top 20 lists. It is very, very difficult to find out how these companies do what they do and their prices seem very low in comparison to other networks. The most popular rumor is that they have some sort of sophisticated Chinese bot net that downloads your app from the app store. This drives your installs. If Apple catches you using one of these networks, they will ban your app or prevent you from getting on the Top 20 list.

The other kind of network might be exemplified by companies like Appia, Flurry or Millennial Media. They are fairly typical performance advertising networks that simply view an installation as another kind of performance product.

One concern many app developers have is that they don't want to install a custom piece of code to allow the network to identify that an application is being used for attribution (called an SDK) for each of these networks, so third party installation vendors such as HasOffers and Ad-X have sprung up that provide a generic SDK with hooks that allow them to receive the notification of installation and then pass that notification to a variety of third party networks. This simplifies the process of working with CPI (Cost Per Install) advertising vendors. Now you can install a single line of code for installation tracking and dozens of potential CPI partners can use it for managing their campaign. Also, they can provide a unified reporting platform and manage de-duplicating conversion credit - You would never want to pay both Appia and

Flurry for showing ads to someone who later installs your app - last ad wins!

The next step in the app install industry is retargeting app users to drive re-engagement. Given that application developers have the device identifier for people that downloaded their app, it is fairly straightforward to target those people on their devices with messages that drive re-engagement around their application. Companies like Dunkin' Donuts, that have invested substantially over the last several years in driving millions of installs will want to advertise to people who have their application installed with deep-linking messages that drive consumers to specific, relevant parts of their application that generate value for the consumer and returns for the corporation. With the investment in marketing made to acquire customers, not driving re-engagement seems short-sighted. Expect sales around re-engagement products to skyrocket in the next few years.

Foot Traffic

Finally, let's talk about the evolving world of attribution for physical locations. If you have a storefront, this kind of attribution is relevant to you. Mobile marketing is revolutionizing advertising - and I don't just mean digital advertising. Mobile marketing is a uniquely personal tool - it is the device that every person has and they carry it with them everywhere they go. They look at it 50 times per day doing a variety of things. When marketers think about mobile advertising, generally they are thinking about location-based targeting. Previously, advertisers felt like they could reach consumers surfing at home or at work. Now they can reach them at the mall, at the Starbucks, at the gas station, or at the grocery store.

Location-based targeting is great (I will talk about it a bunch later), but one of the most exciting aspects of tracking users location is the chance to use it in closed-loop marketing. To the extent that we have shown the user an ad for a retail location (let's say a Best Buy), theoretically, knowledge of a user's location should allow us to identify when that user actually visits this location.

This is a game changer in many ways for retail advertisers. If they can determine that they can pay a certain amount for advertising and then it successfully drives a person into their store, then they are suddenly turning what had felt like unmeasurable advertising into a very measurable experience. McDonald's could know "we showed ads to these people at this location and x percent of them then showed up at the store for lunch the next day". That calculation is the next best thing to counting dollars in an ROI measurement. Furthermore, that data can be turned into consumer intelligence unlike any source of data previously: By observing your mobile device, it is possible to identify your home location (determined by frequent visits to the same place late at night), pull in transactional or census data associated with that location, and inform advertisers of the demographic, psychographic and commercial habits of their consumers on a near individual level at an unprecedented scale.

There are several different ways that mobile advertising companies enable this technology. The first is to rely on ad calls to generate a sample. In the same fashion that they used an ad call to their network to identify the consumer, ascertain their location, and show them a relevant ad, an ad call from the retail location can identify that the consumer visited the location. An obvious shortcoming of this approach is that the only observations you make are when the consumer gets out their phone and triggers an ad that the network can observe. The result is a small sample. While a network can say that they saw 10 people at the retail store, all parties are aware that it is likely a small percentage of the total number of people that visited the store. Unfortunately, there is no way to calculate the actual number of people that visited the store as a result of exposure using this simple model. It is only possible to determine the number of visitors relative to a control group. For example, one could say that 1,000 people were exposed, 10 were later seen at the store and 8 people were later seen at the store that had similar characteristics but were not exposed to the creative message. From this, one could determine the effectiveness of the advertising campaign at generating foot traffic, without understanding how many total people visited the store as a result of the campaign. Now, if an advertiser knew the total number of retail visits, by looking at the total visits observed by the advertising platform, it would be possible to infer advertising effectiveness, however few retailers have strong data in this regard. A number of startups are working hard on helping retailers address this problem, such as RetailNext, Sonic Notify, and Nomi.

Companies like Placed that are active in the mobile attribution space use a panel methodology to circumvent these problems. Placed has an app installed on thousands of consumer's devices that shares with Placed everywhere the consumer goes, regardless of whether they are using the app or not. The result is that Placed can know with certainty that, of their 100,000 installed consumers, 1,000 were exposed to the ad and 200 went to the store subsequently. By scaling up the installed base to the targeted population, it is possible to infer with strong precision the exact number of visits to the retailer generated by the advertising campaign.

The newest and most effective solution to this problem is iBeacons. iBeacons are inexpensive hardware that interfaces with Apple's iOS (There is a similar technology for Android) to invoke events based on proximity. By installing iBeacons in a retail store, when a consumer is proximate to the beacon, an app can send a message indicating its location. For advertising platforms with large app installed bases, this will allow them to count every single individual that visits the stores and uses their apps. The promise of iBeacons for advertisers is nothing short of a revolution in location-based attribution.

CHAPTER 7

Pirates and Math

Meet the Pirates

In the movie adaptation of Glengarry Glen Ross, Alec Baldwin breaks down a classic framework for thinking about the conversion process: Attention, Interest, Decision, Action. AIDA. That is their version of a sales funnel. When you think about the selling process and how that relates back to attribution, you'll want to measure activity at every point in that funnel.

There are many different sales frameworks, but for our purpose I want to use a popular framework that closely aligns with a typical web site or mobile application conversion funnel. This was developed by Dave McClure, former VP of marketing for Paypal and prominent investor, and described as "Startup Metrics for Pirates".[1] Mr. McClure broke the analysis of the conversion process on site into five areas:

- Acquisition
- Activation
- Retention
- Referral
- Revenue

Why pirates? Because pirates say, "AARRR!"

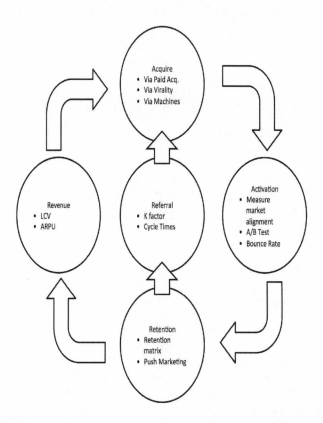

This framework looks at not just selling the customer initially, but the relationship of the customer and the product over time. Each one of these areas can be analyzed and optimized independent of other areas. One of the simplest ways for a startup to think about conversion rate optimization is to study each area. For each metric, there can be assigned a likelihood that it will occur and a value to that occurrence based on the likelihood that it will be associated with revenue.

Similarly, as you drill through each dimension, you should be tracking how different traffic sources behave and segmenting them into cohorts to analyze. Things you might want to look at include:

- Cohorts based on any demographic data or psychographic data you have. (This would be particularly appropriate if you are testing something like Facebook advertising where targeting on this basis is so straightforward.)
- Cohorts based on creative themes (Coupon/Promotional codes, different calls to actions)
- Different landing pages

Facebook's Growth Team used a very similar segmentation model of Acquisition, Activation, and Engagement. eBay had a similar model.

| | | Cohorts | | | |
| | | Search Term A | | Search Term B | |
Measures	Goals	Landing Page A	Landing Page B	Landing Page A	Landing Page B
Acquisition	Page Views	2.6	2.3	4.1	2.2
	Bounce Rate	40.3%	53.0%	29.8%	47.8%
Activation	Uses Feature A	12.5%	13.7%	8.5%	15.9%
	Uses Feature B	8.6%	19.2%	23.0%	19.9%
Retention	3 visits in first week	8.8%	9.1%	12.8%	5.7%
Referral	Referred 2 people	12.0%	25.9%	18.7%	19.9%
	% Referrals that signed up	67.9%	79.9%	69.3%	75.8%
Revenue	Conversion Rate	2.7%	2.9%	5.4%	2.6%
	LCV	$23.00	$28.57	$49.97	$22.75
	Acquisition Cost	$26.94	$26.94	$27.95	$27.95

A framework like this will be critical to both measuring your outcomes and identifying gaps in your revenue engine. The awesome thing about measuring is that it tells you what to do! Work on things where measurement tells you that they aren't working.

Acquisition

The goal of acquisition is to drive customers to your experience. We have talked at a high level about key kinds of customer acquisition engines: growth by brute force, machines, people and paid acquisition. We will talk more about the mechanics of using these when the numbers are poor in a moment, but first let's talk about goals. An example of goals associated with acquisition include total amounts of new visitors. Another goal might be a low bounce rate. (Bounce rate is the percentage of customers that visit one page then leave.) A high bounce rate might indicate that it is low quality traffic.

When LinkedIn was getting started in 2008, they identified three main sources of traffic: email invitations (viral growth; growth by people), search engine optimization ("SEO") results where people landed on profile pages (growth by machines), and homepage views (most likely random PR, LinkedIn did not use paid acquisition as the other techniques are typically more aligned with social network growth). For each of these traffic sources, they identified how many page views each of these generated, what conversions rates were like, and how engaged these users were.[2] That is the level of discipline you need in managing inbound traffic.

When you think about the value of these activities, the value of any incremental visitor is limited. The value of a visit to your business is maybe 1% of the LCV (representing your conversion rate). If you know that 80% of your site traffic leaves after the first page (the bounce rate) and that, of the people that do not bounce, the likelihood that they convert rises dramatically (2%? That is 100% growth!) the implications are significant. Think about it, if you were able to decrease your bounce rate to 60% - a 25% decrease - then your conversion rate would rise 17%. That means improving your bounce rate metrics creates quantifiable incremental value for the business.

By putting a goal or two such as this in place for acquisition, it creates a framework to measure the quality of traffic acquired. At the very top of the funnel as you drive customers to your web site, you want to be tracking for each source of traffic the amount of volume you think it could drive, the price of that traffic and how well it performs.

Activation

Activation is about getting the visitor off the first page and engaged with using the site. Again, here you need a goal or two and I can give you a few examples to get you started. Goals might be spending 30 seconds on the site, generating 5 or more page views, creating an account, or using one of three major features of the site. All of these can indicate that you got the consumers attention. Pick one of these that seems meaningful to your business and get started.

The trick is this: The things you measure should probably look like they aren't working. If they are rosy, you are probably looking at a vanity metric that you should show investors, but not measure yourself on. Lookk is a company that lets people vote on fashion designs. By their original metric, 90% of users activated (by voting)[3]. When they dug deeper, they discovered that the people using the app were not "users" at all. They were friends of designers. When they looked at people who had voted for more than one designer, the numbers fell off a cliff. The activation metric that they needed to measure was slightly less obvious.

I have seen the danger of looking at the wrong vanity metrics with investors in my work advising startups. I worked with a company that produced an iPad app that very early on was featured in the app store. The company used this spike in downloads to demonstrate the popularity of their app, but the problem with this curve was that it leveled off dramatically. While many people downloaded it during that brief period, because the app was not yet optimized for engagement, all of the other metrics stayed flat and the app looked like it stopped growing. Further, all of the work the team was doing was focused on improving engagement, not driving more downloads. They were better served by showing how engagement was increasing over time as they invested in the product than focusing investors on how during one brief period of uncontrolled marketing they received an influx of users. Without repeatability, this marketing did not serve their cause very well.

It should be straightforward to determine the percentage of traffic to your site that engages in these behaviors on their first visit. It's more difficult, but not substantially so, to associate these actions with conversion rates. That is important, so do that work. If you have a freemium product and it reveals that only 3% of people that use one of your major features turn into paying customers, that should tell you something. If 90% of people that use the feature turn into customers, that's a good feature. You need to drive people to that feature for activation. This is a great thing to optimize around.

This is where on-site optimization begins. Let's introduce A/B tests for a moment because we are going to talk about them a lot. In an A/B test, you have two variations ("A" and "B") and you alternate showing them to visitors to see what the difference is in engagement. For example, you may have a headline on your site that says, "Buy One Get One Free" and another headline you are considering that says, "Get A Second Free With Every Purchase" Even though these are making the same offer, it is probably true that the wording of the offer will dramatically effect the consumer engagement around the offer. So you will want to test these headlines to see which performs better. When one definitively wins by producing a result that is significantly better, stop testing and use the best result going forward. This is a classic A/B test. Then you are ready to test the next one!

You should do lots of landing page tests and other A/B tests using Google's Web Site Optimizer or Optimizely. You should try to do a mix of "big changes" because you don't want to find a local maxima when a much higher maxima is inches away and "small changes" to learn. The goal for most of these tests is "how quick can you do them". If it takes you weeks to test something, you should be testing three or four other things in the meantime (simultaneously).

Having said that, you should pick a number of tests appropriate to the size and scale of your organization. If you are a one-man show, it might be difficult to test a dozen things at once and keep the results straight. Also, you need significant results, so you can't shard results across too many cells. Conversely, you are a startup. You need to rise up and do more than you think you are capable of. This is the true spirit of the entrepreneur.

A key metric at early Facebook was that they had determined that people who had 7 friends in the first 10 days of use were substantially more active on the site than people that did not. The result was that Facebook formed a tiger team that worked to ensure that more people reached that goal. This was a great example of growth hacking that powered tremendous user activation and retention at Facebook. Without effective measurement and regression analysis of user behavior, this key engagement behavior would never be recognized and optimized.

Activation and Retention should be the starting point for really measuring effectiveness. While people that pick up a book like this are inclined to focus in on acquisition and revenue, that is not the best place to start. The first thing to work on is making sure users have a great experience. If the first hundred consumers have a bad experience, what is the value of sending a million consumers to your site? If everyone leaves right away, how high can your LCV really be?

The takeaway from this statement might be "I should focus on retention", and that isn't terrible, but to start with, activation is a great place to begin. If you aren't activating people, then you won't have the data to test retention properly. Furthermore, you might be attracting the wrong customers. **Activation is how you test market alignment.**

Let's spend a few moments deep-diving on bounce rate – an excellent metric for activation. Bounce rate is the percentage of visitors that leave after looking at one page. Frequently, this is indicative of how effective that first page is at engaging a consumer. Certainly, for many business models, bounce rate is a poor metric – some sites are designed for people to come, get what they need and leave. Wikipedia has a high bounce rate, its goals focus more on turning consumers into editors.

Generally speaking, bounce rate is an easily measured, effective tool for looking at acquisition.[6] There are several ways that bounce rate can be used.

- **Measure bounce rate at the landing page level:** Many people will arrive at your site through a door other than the home page thanks to the deep-linking power of Google search. For that matter, you may have custom landing pages for your marketing campaigns. Understand the bounce rate of each. Think about the best practices associated with your best performing pages and how those can be transferred across your site.

- **Measure bounce rate at the referrer level:** Here you can see who is sending you traffic and how well that performs. This speaks to both traffic quality and the resonance between what you are doing and how you are positioned vis-a-vis the site that is sending you traffic.

- **Measure bounce rate at the keyword level or Facebook audience:** This is real, on-the-ground data that gives you insight into your power terms in a search context. If you

---

6. And it is in Google Analytics right out of the box.

see search terms that cause your bounce rate to plummet, that indicates high alignment with an audience that you can exploit. That is, here is an audience that is actively clicking through, but not engaging with your content. Landing page improvements could turn this around.

- **Cohort analysis** may be appropriate as well. You might want to compare long-time users to new users.

Retention

We have successfully engaged a customer on their first visit. Now we need to get them back. Only by getting them back can we turn interest into habits. And you deserve to be a habit! This is what retention is about. We need them to think about us all the time.

Retention is not just visited again, it is about getting the user back and engaged around some core activity to the system. We don't want them to read yet another blog post about our photo app. We want them to take a photo! If we can't get them back after their first use, we are letting the team down.

Obviously, the best kind of retention mechanisms are core to the product and teach the client they need to come back regularly. A great example of retention design is looking at great mid-core games such as Clash of Clans, the number one revenue-generating iOS game for more than a year. The objective of mid-core games is to engender just this sort of habit building. They recognize that mid-core game players love games but are busy, so they attempt to build a mechanic that allows them to play in five minute bursts. The concern is that if they leave, they might not come back. So here is what SuperCell (the maker of Clash of Clans) does to "teach" people to come back:

First, they make you leave! When your army is destroyed, there is nothing for you to do while your army rebuilds. They tell you "hey, this is a time when you can go do other things." Initially, the wait times are very short. You start with weak troops that can be built quickly. You leave for 5 minutes, then get to attack again! So the first one hundred times you leave, you know that you are supposed to come right back. Slowly, as your troops become more powerful, it takes longer to build them and they stretch that window to thirty minutes or an hour. Similarly, you start with very weak resource collectors that allow you to build a more powerful base. If you don't "collect" from them frequently, they will fill up and not generate new resources. Finally, you have builders, who use resources collected to build new offensive and defensive weapons for you. Initially, the things that the builders create may take 15 minutes. Over time, they may take as long as a week or two.

All of these game mechanics are designed with specific mid-core retention mechanics in mind. The objective SuperCell has is to train your mind to check in frequently. If you have 10 minutes, stop by and attack someone with your army. If you have 2 minutes, stop by and collect resources or get a builder busy. If you don't, you may be attacked by other players and have your resources stolen! Initially, you can stop by almost any time you want - it only takes 10 minutes to build a new army. Over time, things take longer to build, but they are more expensive as well, so managing resources is critical. Also, as you mature, you may join a "clan" where peer pressure from fellow players creates a community that requires frequent interaction using tools like a troop sharing mechanic.

Finally, SuperCell makes sure to send a wave of notifications reminding you that your troops are ready to fight, that you haven't visited your clan in some period of time, and other alerts to drive re-engagement.

There are generally more broad tools used by many organizations to facilitate lightweight retention and keep their service top of mind. Maybe it is a blog. Maybe it is a periodic email. Retention mechanisms that are fairly common include various kinds of emails:

- Weekly or monthly status emails
- Lifecycle emails are drip marketing emails sent a few days after joining and a few weeks after joining
- Event-based emails that are sent after they do something on the site

One of the more common and effective techniques that is presently in vogue for start-ups is the faux-founder email. Expensify is a great example of a company that used this in the early going and the CEO, David Barrett, told me that he received responses to nearly every email that the system sent out. Thirty to sixty minutes after the consumer signs up (randomizing the time slightly around 30 minutes is helpful if you want to be just like Expensify), they get an automated "real email from the founder" that speaks colloquially, invites them to contact the founder with questions, and engages them in a meaningful dialog. This "human touch" is very compelling at connecting a consumer to a start-up and can dramatically improve retention and engagement.

David Barrett <smtp30@expensify.com>   11/12/09
to me

Hi there! I see you just signed up for Expensify, welcome! Can you tell me about yourself? Namely, what
sort of work do you do, how big is your company, how do you currently do expense reports, how did you
learn about Expensify, how do you hope to use it -- that sort of thing. Thanks!

-david
Founder and CEO of Expensify
Follow us here: http://twitter.com/expensify

SproutSocial uses a different sign-up strategy, sending a plain text email welcoming you and showing you how to log in immediately after you join and then a few hours later, dripping another email to you offering webinars and doing features and benefits.

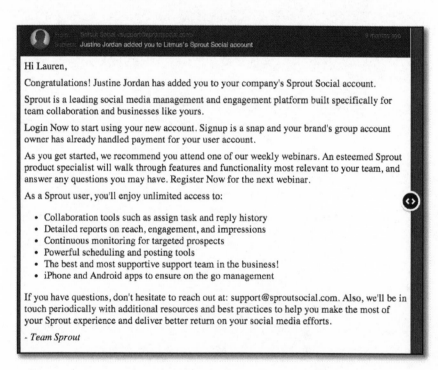

Justine Jordan added you to Litmus's Sprout Social account

Hi Lauren,

Congratulations! Justine Jordan has added you to your company's Sprout Social account.

Sprout is a leading social media management and engagement platform built specifically for team collaboration and businesses like yours.

Login Now to start using your new account. Signup is a snap and your brand's group account owner has already handled payment for your user account.

As you get started, we recommend you attend one of our weekly webinars. An esteemed Sprout product specialist will walk through features and functionality most relevant to your team, and answer any questions you may have. Register Now for the next webinar.

As a Sprout user, you'll enjoy unlimited access to:

- Collaboration tools such as assign task and reply history
- Detailed reports on reach, engagement, and impressions
- Continuous monitoring for targeted prospects
- Powerful scheduling and posting tools
- The best and most supportive support team in the business!
- iPhone and Android apps to ensure on the go management

If you have questions, don't hesitate to reach out at: support@sproutsocial.com. Also, we'll be in touch periodically with additional resources and best practices to help you make the most of your Sprout experience and deliver better return on your social media efforts.

- Team Sprout

Welcome emails are very effective. Studies have shown that they are opened four times more frequently than other email messages and clicked on five times more often[4]. That is significant, so executing a good welcome email strategy is meaningful.

MailChimp uses a different drip marketing strategy. Every three days for the first two weeks after you join, they send you a different standard email talking about best practices for using their product. This reflects their engagement and retention mechanisms: They want you to be successful using their product to ensure you become a paying customer and they want to get you into the product a few times in the first two weeks doing specific activities. So each email is about a different part of their system that you should optimize for success.

One last type of event email worth mentioning is the "One day after you join" email. If you drip to customers an email 24 hours after they join asking them how their first day with you was, you will get responses. JotForm uses this so effectively that they have to disable it from time to time because they get so many responses that customer support is overwhelmed.

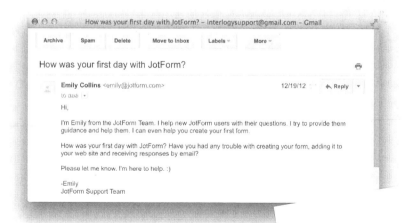

Retention and activation are the starting point for your optimization journey. If you sign up 100 people and retain none of them then your LCV will be terrible. When you first get started, having churn above 10% per month occurs frequently, but that merely symbolizes that you are not really ready for a wave of customers. At 10% monthly churn, in a few months they would all be gone. And what's worse is when you lose someone, generally, they are gone forever. It needs to be under 2% before you really start acquiring customers. In 2011, Pacific Crest surveyed SaaS businesses about churn rates and more than 75% had an annual churn rate below 5%.[5] If you are targeting SMBs, conventional wisdom is an annual churn rate of 15% is good (1.17% monthly)[6].

For the purposes of this kind of analysis, you will want to build a retention matrix:

Weekly Cohort	People	Week 2	Week 3	Week 4	Week 5	Week 6	Week 7
Oct 2	1023	15.4%	12.8%	10.6%	7.5%	6.4%	5.7%
Oct 9	989	13.7%	11.9%	9.8%	8.4%	7.1%	5.8%
Oct 16	1057	14.6%	11.7%	10.2%	7.9%	6.8%	6.1%
Oct 23	1313	12.8%	10.9%	10.0%	7.5%	6.4%	5.9%
Oct 30	1512	12.9%	11.5%	9.1%	7.8%	6.6%	
Nov 5	981	12.8%	11.4%	9.5%	8.3%		
Nov 12	899	13.1%	9.8%	9.1%			
Nov 19	1212	13.0%	10.1%				

This matrix helps you identify the effect of changes you make to your platform in terms of platform stickiness. When you make a change, you hope that it makes people use your platform. Those changes should show up here.

If you have a MRR kind of business (monthly recurring revenue), you will obviously look at straightforward customer churn. But you need to dive much deeper than that to improve the experience. You need to understand the composition of the churn. In the early going, churn rate will be hard to measure. You need to think about other things to measure while you wait for churn numbers to begin to emerge. How many times people come back in a month? How many people engage in those emails? We should be testing and optimizing when we send emails to maximize re-engagement. We should be testing how frequently someone needs to come to the site to turn the site into their habit. Is it three times per week? Five times per month? Both?

Think about the user as well. At LinkedIn, they discovered that retention emails for active users were very different than retention emails for inactive users.[7] The result was that different messages were crafted for different audiences. Studying the characteristics of users that stay compared to users that churn is critical to making the product improvements that will help retain customers and reduce churn.

People rarely "leave" when they leave. Particularly in MRR businesses. People generally "leave" in their minds months before and then you do something that reminds them to unsubscribe. This is part of why strong cohort analytics around usage patterns are so important - people leave at different times for different reasons, so looking at a single blended number will lead you astray.

If they stop using the product early, it could be poor onboarding and tutorials or a poor hook. If they stop using it after the first few weeks, it could be that your game is not deep enough. After a few months, it could have been an update that went poorly or the lack of an update.

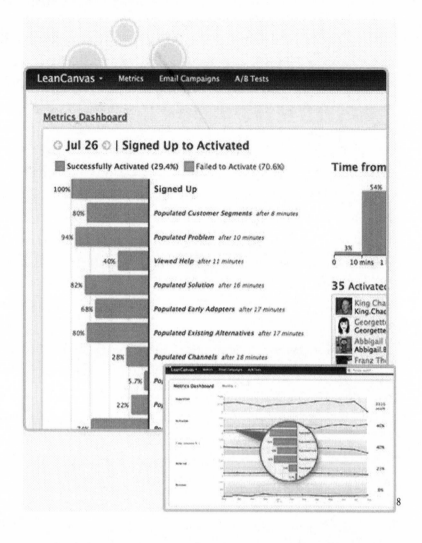

In a SaaS business, one technique that can pay dividends is simply sending customers who sign up for the monthly plan a coupon to sign up for the annual plan after they have been on the monthly plan for 30 days. Similarly, in eCommerce, what we typically do when we think about retention is think about driving reorders. Coupons and discounts are a common mechanism for re-engaging valuable customers that already have a relationship with your site.

Every company is different. Two sided marketplaces have the same dynamic, but you are forced to measure all of these metrics on both sides of the market.

Finally, I have a pearl of wisdom in this regard: Much of the churn that happens on Internet-based MRR sites and subscription products in general (5% customer churn per year, on average!) is simply expired credit cards. The accepted best practice is to notify customers 2 weeks in advance of expiration to get them to update it. I would go one step further: You should be checking 10 weeks before expiration to make sure they are engaged. Have your support team reach out. Engage them pro-actively. You don't want this to be the signal to cancel your service. You want to re-engage them on the platform 75 days before expiration if they have disengaged to ensure that you seamlessly transition. This is a productive area for A/B testing a variety of messages and tweaks when you are focused on reducing long term churn. The good news is that it will be easy to see when credit card expirations become a meaningful part of the churn composition.

Referral

Now that the customer is engaged, they need to share it with the world. If we didn't talk about making things viral memes, we wouldn't be doing it right.

<Insert captioned picture of kittens here.>

Your business deserves to be a viral meme on the lips of all of your potential customers and it is up to your existing customers to help you spread the word.

I won't lie, some businesses just ain't that interesting, but as this is at the core of the growth by people meme, it is worth spending a fair bit of time thinking about how you can engage your own customers to spread the word about your product. There are only a few ways that a company can grow, and this isn't appropriate to most companies, but it is so powerful that it is important to think about how it can be applied to your business. Word of mouth is powerful and the growth of the social Internet has only made it more so. Instead of telling a neighbor, when someone spreads the word they tell their 3,000 closest friends. That is pretty good stuff.

We will talk about virality in much more detail in a bit, but let's start by talking about why it's important in the context of what we have been discussing. Imagine two identical businesses. One is getting $20 in LCV per customer, has no referral engine, and hence is paying up to $19.99 for a customer to be acquired. Not unreasonable. Unfortunately, their competitor has a similar cost structure of $20 LCV, but 50% of their customers refer a future customer who has a customer acquisition cost of $0. Suddenly, the LCV they could invest in marketing is $30. Now they are offering $25 for customers and are generating higher profit margins and have captured the entire market. So referrals can level up even paid acquisition and sales force based strategies.

Now imagine that every customer refers two customers that sign up. In the lingo, which we will discuss, this is called having a K factor greater than 1. It also means you are winning big time. Now you don't spend any money on customer acquisition. You just knock down the first domino and all the other dominos fall down.

To create an environment of referrals, you might have some sort of sharing mechanism with discounts for both parties, you might run contests or campaigns of some sort, and you might have some sort of email or widgets that facilitate letting the world know what happy customers they are. The best sort of referral strategies revolve around referral being baked into the social nature of the product. This is why social networks rely on growth by people so heavily as a strategy. Take OMGPop's "Draw Something" for example: in order to play the game, you have to get friends to play with you. If it's a utility, find social equivalents: sharing notes with colleagues, tweeting app activity, publishing accomplishments, highlighting insights. This draws in people using an indirect referral model where their use and sharing endorses your product to their peers.

A more broadly applicable example is DropBox. They allow a user to refer a new customer and when the new customer signs up, they both get incrementally more space added to their account than if the new customer had signed up independently. The result is that DropBox created an army of advocates rushing to sign their friends up for DropBox before their friends discovered the service on their own. Customers were incented by the reward of extra room in their account to actively engage their friends. A powerful tool and a productive one for DropBox. As long as the space they gave each account cost less than the average acquisition cost of a customer (and disk is cheap!), these referrals were incredibly effective.

A close friend of mine actually ran a Google Adwords campaign to drive traffic to his affiliate link. This is a person paying money to sign up customers for DropBox so he can get a little more disk space - an essentially free commodity to the DropBox team.

AirBnB recently re-engineered their referral mechanic to increase bookings and their effort was a perfect example of how an operation like this works. First, they defined the metrics they wanted to measure to identify referral success and built technology to track these metrics:

- Monthly Active Users sending Invites
- Invitees per Inviter
- Conversion Rate to New User
- Conversion Rate to New Guest
- Conversion Rate to New Host

Then they tested mechanics and offers to drive referrals and tested email messages that offered the referrer money (self-centered) and allowed the referrer to give discounts to the referee (altruistic). They saw much better performance using the altruistic message and between message improvements and mechanical improvements, increased referral conversions 300%.[9]

In terms of metrics, the most important metric is frequency of sharing and effectiveness – how many referrals actually result in site visits. If sharing is high and effectiveness is low, you can A/B test to optimize that. More interestingly, tracking conversion rates for this cohort is important. They may convert at a much higher rate than "cold" customers. Optimization in their conversion path may be extremely valuable to the business and should be monitored.

Revenue

Revenue is where the rubber meets the road. You should know your conversion rates and your LCV. You should know your churn rate. If you don't, go back to the beginning of this book and start over.

I watch "Shark Tank" on television frequently and one thing that always confounds me is when a startup comes into the Shark Tank and doesn't have the answer to average revenue per user (ARPU) and cost of goods sold (COGS) right on the tip of their tongue. If you aren't good with numbers, you need to get good. Winning is math. You need to love the math. When those entrepreneurs on Shark Tank say, "I'm not good at math", my reaction is always, "And they think someone should give them money when they confess they aren't good at counting money?" Those people always walk away from the sharks empty handed. Ignorance of revenue and profits is ignorant. Nobody wants to bet that ignorant people will be successful. Don't be that person.

Notes

1. http://500hats.typepad.com/500blogs/2007/09/startup-metrics.html
2. http://quibb.com/links/lessons-learned-from-growing-linkedin-to-175-million-users
3. http://www.slideshare.net/andreasklinger/startup-metrics-a-love-story?
4. https://litmus.com/blog/sprout-socials-welcome-email-makes-a-good-first-impression

5. http://www.pacificcrest-
news.com/saas/Pacific%20Crest%202011%20SaaS%20Workshop.
pdf
6. http://blog.hopkins.io/2014/03/20/churn/
7. https://www.blossom.io/blog/2012/11/01/growth-hackers-
conference-lessons-learned.html
8. http://usercycle.com/assets/home/cohort_analysis_410-
e1bbe864ece2706ff9123e588262c814.png
9. http://nerds.airbnb.com/making-referrals-work-for-airbnb/

CHAPTER 8

Work Backwards From Your Product

How Do I Track?

Now we know how attribution works in theory and we have thought critically about the things that are important for us to measure. When you do acquire a new customer, I cannot emphasize the importance of placing people into the right cohorts and tracking their performance. Understanding where your traffic is coming from and how that traffic performs once it gets to your site is essential to success.

For example, casual gaming sites are notorious for having incredibly high click-through rates because the ads are placed in positions where an accidental click is likely. The traffic driven by these inventory sources typically performs poorly for most post-click activity (however, it might perform well for downloading more casual games), so understanding what happens on-site for various forms of traffic is important.

Once, I saw huge click-through rates (7%+) on an iPhone app that we had bought some traffic on. When I investigated, it turned out that it was a flashlight app and in all likelihood, people were clicking the ad when they were trying to turn on the flashlight in the dark. This is both worst case user experience for the app and it performed terribly for me on the backend as well. No one who is in a pitch black room trying to work a flashlight is wondering where the nearest Buffalo Wild Wings is. That is not an opinion, that is actually a fact that I have proven via testing.

You probably want to use an off-the-shelf third party tool to handle this, but for ninety percent of cases, free Google Analytics is adequate. If you are using mobile apps, Flurry is a similar product in this area. There are many others: KISSMetrics, MixPanel, Omniture, and other. But I recommend starting simple and free and keeping it lean.

There are four kinds of things you are interested in measuring:

Usability: This is task direction. You can get some of this through extensive path analysis on Google Analytics. You can also use something like usertesting.com to get more feedback. Companies like Aol bring people in and observe them physically navigate the site using directed tests. You probably don't need that. That is Rolls Royce style. We just need to get from Point A to Point B. For the kind of work you are doing, you probably don't need usertesting.com, either. Now, if you are trying to figure out if your product is good, having users try using your product while you observe them might be really helpful, but for conversion rate optimization in the early going, it might be overkill. Casual testing is fun and interesting, but the sample size required for real testing is probably prohibitive at the earliest (MVP) stage of your business.

Quantitative: This is Google Analytics sweet spot. This is just raw measurement of traffic and user engagement. It should tell you what users are doing and how they spend their time on your site. Conversion rates and other metrics are found here.

Comparative: This is your cohort analysis, your A/B and your multivariate tests. Copy, colors, graphics, and hopefully much more interesting things are constantly being baked off. If you deploy them properly, you can use Google Analytics and similar tools to help you get this done. If you have money and it is burning a hole in your pocket, you could buy specialized tools for this such as Optimizely and you will surely say, "How did I live without these tools!" They are specialized tools and in that respect work very well at what they do.

Competitive: You should be tracking competitors and what they do. This is a different class of tools that are indirectly measuring things that may or may not be of interest to you, but you need be thinking about what you can and want to measure here. There are simple versions of this like Alexa and the tools you can use in Google Adwords for free. There are also very complex versions of these tools such as SpyFu, Quantcast, and Compete.com. You should definitely not spend money on this category of tools until you really are ramping acquisition and you feel like you are competing for customers in your marketing spend. Having said that, you should know what your competitors are doing and understand how your strategy and their strategy intersect.

A Million Ways to Enter, But You Can Never Leave

You might start out with your home page as the primary landing page you drive traffic to, but you will find it very effective if you start to build out custom landing pages for your audiences.

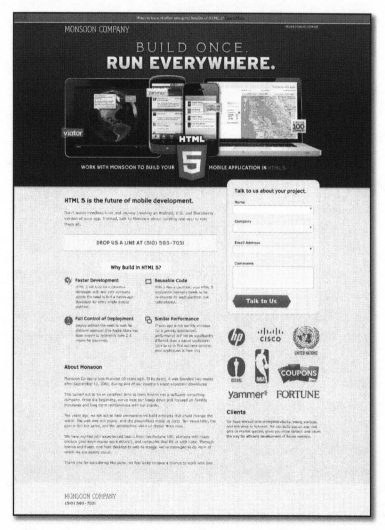

1

Landing pages allow you to customize your message for incoming visitors. This means that you can continue the message that you started with your ads, which creates a cohesive experience. As you test new creative messages and attract different audiences as a result of those messages, leveraging the context of the creative pays dividends on the landing page.

These custom landing pages also allow you to direct visitors toward specific actions that further their engagement with your brand, such as downloading a free ebook. (Displaying traditional navigation may distract your visitors.)

Finally, landing pages make tracking post-click engagement much easier. They can also simplify testing messaging. Landing pages are the perfect place for you to A/B test ad effectiveness. Everyone, including myself, proselytizes the value of A/B tests, but you can't test everything in the early going. Don't worry about button colors. Test things that you think matter. You can do all the tests when you have hundreds of thousands of visitors per month. To get results for your tests, you need a significant volume of outcomes. The more tests you are doing, the more traffic you need to drive significant outcomes. Use your landing pages to test the things that you believe will most significantly move the needle.

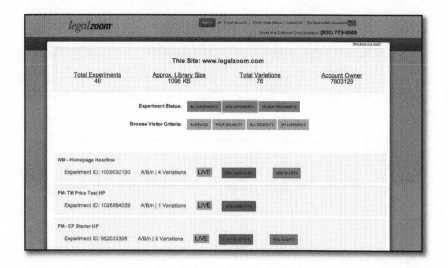

Here I used some special code to scrape the experiments that LegalZoom is conducting on their home page. You can see that their first three tests are the headline, the pricing, and the "hero image" offering a special wizard tool. Big value pieces on their homepage are a key area of focus. Of course, LegalZoom gets a lot of traffic so they can run many tests and test many variations simultaneously and not worry about struggling to get their results to significance.

Anyone that spends time googling A/B tests will hear a story about how changing a button color from blue to green increased conversions 57% or some such. There is a reason those stories are so amazing; it almost never happens. It is the exception, not the rule. There is no doubt that by tweaking colors and shapes and fonts and position of a button on a page, you can find a million things that move the needle a tiny bit. It is unlikely that any of those move the needle dramatically. Focus on the things that you think will be game changers. Don't get sucked into playing the local maxima game.

More tests is better though. The more you are testing, the more you are learning and that directly relates to growth. Here is a slide that the head of product at Twitter shares with people that correlates Twitter growth and the amount of A/B tests they were conducting each week:

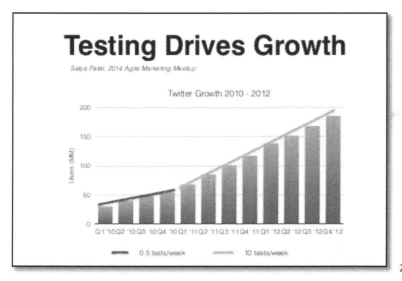

2

Now, I suspect there is some confounding data here. As I indicated previously, there is a limit to the number of tests that one can conduct until scale is reached. Further, Twitter may have reached a business inflection point and entered a tornado of growth unrelated to testing, but the fact that leadership highlights this shift speaks to the potential value.

But I Learned So Much About Attribution

It feels like we have talked for hundreds of pages about attribution. What is our attribution strategy? Unfortunately, I don't think the purpose of your startup is to fix the attribution problem. Most of these industry-standard tools are going to focus on last click, and last click is obviously inaccurate, not crediting interactions further up the funnel, but last click is probably not completely terrible. Furthermore, it is unlikely that you are investing heavily in branding and brand advertising, so there is little or no need to worry about top-of-funnel kinds of marketing and how that is driving overall value in our marketing mix. If everything we are doing is bottom of the funnel, the mix of marketing that a consumer is exposed to should be minimal and the discounting of "brand"-ish activities won't concern us.

Google Analytics, a tool that will most likely represent a key weapon in your arsenal, has a multi-channel attribution model built in that shows "assisted conversions" and "last click" conversions. This is a lightweight model, but it can help inform your decision making in this regard.

Frankly, when the time comes for a more complex model, you will know it. Also, you will have exhausted all of the advice in this book. The only complexity we will add to our measurement of the marketing mix will be cohort analysis.

One Way to Nerd Out on Cohort Analysis

This is getting pretty far down in the weeds, but I am a believer that winning the marketing and analytics battle will probably involve building your own databases at a certain point. Given that, I want to walk through an example of how you could build your own database and think about cohort retention.

The approach for this database is a simple model that is a collection of UserIDs-CookieIDs/Timestamps/Events.[7] When a person on your site does something, you log an ID that you assign them (via a Cookie), the time they did it, and the name of the event in this table. It's that easy. Frankly, this is not significantly different than what some commercial products charge a fair bit of money to do for you.

You have an event for "registered". This allows you to query your database and pull all of the people that registered in the last two days. You have an event for "Came from SEO". Maybe you have another table where you log extra event information like the SEO term, but lets keep it simple for right now. So you can pull all of the users who came from SEO vs. Organic in the last two days. You should log an event like "Logged In". Now you could write a simple query that says "For everyone who registered in the last 30 days, show me how many people logged in 3x and whether their source was SEO vs. Organic". You could then pull it for the 30 days prior and compare. You could log an event that says "Showed them homepage A" or "homepage B", then see how that affects

---

7. For most databases, you will want to have lots of rows, not lots of columns. You don't want to have a column for every event, you want to just create more and more rows. That is typically much faster.

retention and build your own A/B split testing infrastructure. A data structure like this is the low hanging fruit of cohort analysis.

When people say "growth hacking is the future", all they really mean is that being able to get into the weeds like this is where you find out the truth. An ability to think about how you want to capture this data, access this data, and realize the kinds of questions that you can ask with this data are the essence of growth hacking. Remember our unofficial motto: "Being close to the iron is where innovation really happens!"

Price Matters

Building a great product is great, but optimization for revenue is important also. Let's be clear: If your product isn't great, it won't work. I don't want to fly in the face of conventional Lean Start-up wisdom. It should be an MVP: Minimum Viable Product. If it doesn't embarrass you when you ship it, then you waited too long to ship it. I believe all these things to be true. But let's be clear what that means. You should have a vision of absolute brilliance that completely solves someone's problem. Your product should not be that complete fulfillment when you ship it. It should do the one thing that most fulfills your customers needs. But it needs to do it amazingly. That one aspect of your product needs to be polished to a brilliant sheen. If using that one feature that your product has when it ships does not make people love your baby, then your baby is doomed.

The reason everyone tells you that you need to get out quickly with your product and be lean and do customer development is because you are probably wrong about everything. You ship quickly with an MVP to find out if that one feature is valuable to customers. If it isn't, the sooner you know, the sooner you know. But no different than this is the revenue model. Your revenue model is probably wrong. Your price points are wrong. Your pricing approach is wrong.

All of this needs to be tested and validated. The sooner you start, the sooner you know. If you price too high, you limit you market and lower your conversion rates. If you price too low then you don't generate enough LCV and can't afford to acquire customers. This will require testing. You don't want to wait to do this work until you have tons of demand. Then you will be spending time fixing these problems when you could be generating revenue. Split testing price points is one of the most important things you can do in optimizing conversion rates and LCV.

Final Thoughts on the Experience

This is not a book about how to make your site or app's user experience awesome. There are many, many books about that. But I have a few ideas since you are here and this is the book you are (wisely!) reading.

Conversion Rate Optimization begins with walking through the experience and thinking about it from a consumer point of view. The first things consumers think about when they get to the site are:

- **Is the call to action clear and easy to find?** A strong call to action makes a huge difference in the performance of banner ads. Making it obvious on the site what you want consumers to do is equally critical to the success and failure of your business. Banner ads with a big button that says "Click Here" on it are far more likely to get clicked. There is something fundamentally hard-wired into our DNA that makes us want to push buttons.

- **Does your site demonstrate social proof and traction?** Customer testimonials and other indicators that many other non-foolish people are using your tool are a powerful indicator of a product's legitimacy. There is a reason that books have quotes from famous people on the back cover. They use that as third party validation. Do you need third party validation to help get people over the purchase hump?

- **Does your site build trust?** Without trust, there can be no relationship between you and your user. This means commitments around security and confidentiality. Think of the security commitments made on eCommerce sites and the promises of "no spam" on start-up account creation pages. This means professional graphics.

You can install tools like CrazyEgg or use Google Analytics to understand where consumers spend time on your landing pages and at various points in your funnel. This will allow you to confirm that you are focusing consumer attention on the right places.

The battle for attention doesn't end when you get the customer to your experience.

Notes

1. http://unbounce.com/landing-page-examples-built-with-unbounce/

2. http://www.slideshare.net/tractionconf/morgan-brown-coauthor-growth-engines-high-tempo-testing

CHAPTER 9

Growth by Machines: Win The SEO Battle

The Leanest Way to Acquire Customers is not to Spend

We have talked about conversion rate optimization and how to improve the likelihood that a visitor to your experience undertakes the kinds of actions that are the objective of the experience, be it playing the game, buying the product, or subscribing to something.

It is finally time to dive into building sustainable engines of growth. We will start with search engine optimization (SEO) because there is a fundamental set of things that every company should do to maximize their underlying SEO, so regardless of your primary growth engine, you should do the right thing when it comes to SEO. In the big scheme of things, it is a bunch of little adjustments you should make to how you think about building applications and content and once you have those in your head, you are positioned to reap much of the benefits that can accrue from Google driving customers to your site.

If you are a highly ranked organic result in Google for key search terms, this can be a tremendous driver of traffic. Unfortunately, it is slow. There is no SEO strategy that results in instant traffic, however the long-term benefits of a sound SEO strategy make this the next logical step after building an analytics framework for generating traffic to a site or application. Furthermore, if we invest in traffic driving strategies, it is likely that awareness of our site will rise and this is typically correlated with more affection from the Google-machine. If we are going to start attracting more organic search traffic, it makes sense to consider things we could do to make sure that we get the maximum boost possible from Google. This is an area where you can, to some degree, set it and forget it, but beware: Screwing up your SEO right out of the gate diminishes long term traffic, while doing it right enhances it. Hence let's talk about how to do it right.

The first question to ask is: are people currently searching for keywords that closely match the product or service I provide? If so, can I reasonably expect that by designing a site using Google best practices that I could rank at the top for any keywords that in aggregate would drive a meaningful amount of new customers? If not, skip to the next chapter, but consider that if this market is obviously very competitive, you may need additional differentiation, or you may need to segment the market differently. If the way you think about the market is reflected in the search habits of people and you don't think that people will search for terms that describe you and that you can win, you may have chosen a poor market.

If you've done much conversion optimization, you should have observed that things at the top of a page get clicked much more than things lower on the page, all else being equal. SEO is a winner-take-most game: for a given search term, the vast majority of the benefits flow to the handful of sites at the top of the first page. When AOL released data around search activity, the top result received over 40% of the clicks, the second result 11.9%, and so on.[1] The entire second page, by comparison, received only 10%.

This means that winning at the keyword game involves balancing two variables:

- Keywords you can win: If you select keywords such as "search engine optimization" or "mortgage refinance", you are going after very popular keywords that are being actively optimized by literally thousands of skilled professionals with vast resources. You have to pick keywords that are sufficiently niche that other people are not actively attempting to win those keywords. Terms that are both directly related to what you are doing, but somewhat obscure to the general public are a perfect choice in this regard. This speaks to your differentiation in the market. If you are undifferentiated in a competitive market, that is probably a problem.

- Keywords with volume: Winning a game where there is no prize isn't that great. Picking a keyword that no one ever searches for serves you poorly. You have to pick a keyword that has a prize associated with it: traffic. Once again, if you are differentiated in a way that no one cares about, that has broad implications for your market success.

Balancing the need to find words that are not being actively SEO'd by better capitalized competitors and finding terms that are sufficiently active that victory has value is the essence of the strategic planning aspect of SEO.

Even if you have a broad consumer start-up, you still have to pick a first bowling pin to target in this regard. When you tell people your customer is "everybody", it sounds like your target market is "nobody". Figure out where your market starts and go after them.

Pick a Term, Any Term

There are many ways to identify the keywords you intend to target in SEO planning, but I want to spend a few moments illustrating one way to think about the problem.

First, we need to identify a possible list of terms. For a project like this, Google provides excellent tools to customers that are buying keywords via AdWords. It is definitely worth it (because it is free) to have an AdWords account and be using their tools.

In this example, I have used Cogmap, the organization chart wiki and my pet project web site, as an example. I go to the Keyword Planner tool in AdWords and enter "organization chart wiki". The keyword planner tool returns a list of "related terms", search volume for those terms, and an internal Google-powered barometer of competitiveness in bidding for those terms.

It is likely that the competitiveness of bidding for terms is high-ly correlated with interest in the SEO of a term. Regardless, I found that for that term, there were no terms with both high vol-ume and low competition. I then tried just "organization chart" and found a hit.

"Organizational Structure" has several thousand requests per month and low competition. That seems like a term I could win. I record that in my spreadsheet. Repeat this exercise several times until you have 5 to 10 candidate terms.

Once you have a good list of target candidates, get a better sense of their competitiveness. You should go search for them in Google, Bing, and any other popular search engines. (Or just Google, if that is how you want to roll.[8]) Understanding which websites already rank for your keyword gives you valuable insight into the competition, and also how hard it will be to rank for the given term.

Visit the sites at the top. Study them a bit. You have to be better at that term than they are. The goal for Day One is to pick the best term and win it. Remember, there is no prize for second place. In fact, winning second place in a bunch of races is not as good as winning first place in one race. If you are not in the top three listings in the search results for the keyword, you will not reap any of the benefits for ranking for that keyword. So pick one keyword and win it. Pick a good one.

In one study, they looked at a sample of keywords over a 30 day period and tracked click-through rate for various positions. What they saw confirmed our understanding, which was that being in the top two or three positions was necessary to generate traffic.

---

8. We are believers in Occam's Razor!

Click Through Rate by Position

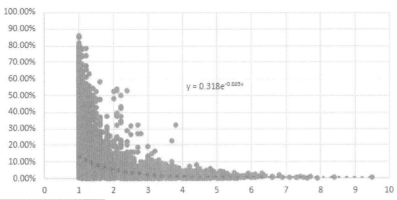

Average Position	CTR
1	12.2%
1.5	4.3%
2	1.5%
2.5	0.5%
3	0.2%
3.5	0.1%
4	0.0%
5	0.0% [2]

If you have narrowed it down to two or three that seem both winnable and overflowing with tasty traffic, then you are in a good place. Now it is possible to do one last test and figure out if that term is really helpful. Our keyword generation has been more art than science up to this point. Bringing some science in and testing the efficacy of that keyword is the last step in our strategy. Fortunately, this can be done concurrently with the conversion rate optimization work that was discussed earlier in the book. To test the efficacy of the keyword, buy a sample campaign for the keyword at Google AdWords and/or the Bing Adcenter. In Google Adwords, choose "exact match", then track impressions and conversion rate over the course of a few hundred clicks. This is where the rubber meets the road because we are testing the alignment of traffic and your message. Keywords that drive traffic but fail to convert customers are literally DOA.

From this, you can determine the exact value of the keyword to you. Calculate the RPM (revenue per 1000 impressions) and combine that with the keyword planners information about average traffic per keyword. From there, you can arrive at a loose approximation of the value of ranking number one for a keyword to your site.

	Volume	Imps	Clicks	Convs	CVR	RPM	Rev Opp
Term A	8,000	1,200	301	3	1.0%	$250.00	2,000.00
Term B	10,000	1,500	308	2	0.6%	$133.33	$1,333.33
Term C	12,000	2,011	321	5	1.6%	$248.63	$2,983.00

For example, if your search ad generated 10,000 impressions, of which 100 visitors have come to your site and 2 have converted for a LCV of $100, then a single visitor for that keyword has an RPM of $1. If you get to the number one position for that keyword, you could expect CTRs as high as 35%.

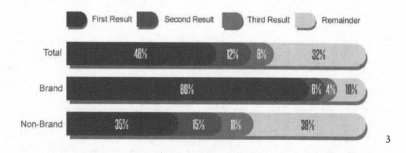

3

So, if you have a keyword that could generate 15,000 impressions per month, and 1/3 of those impressions resulted in traffic to your site, in our example, "winning" that keyword has a value of ~$5,000 per month with essentially no cost.

With this data, we can measure how invested in our SEO strategy we should be and make smart decisions about evolving our SEO strategy.

SEO like a Pro

Search Engine Optimization has a downside. It can go on forever. In picking your optimization approach, an important aspect is to time box it and limit the amount of time you spend on SEO to correlate with the value you expect to extract from SEO. There are many SEO professionals that spend all day doing SEO 24x7. You should not let this be you. The key to winning is to exploit the Pareto Principle and find the 20% of the work that extracts 80% of the value. Fortunately, this industry is conducive to such a plan. Despite what "social media experts" may say, you don't need tons of blogging and tweeting to get 80% of value.

Of course, before I dismiss all of that out of hand, let me speak to its value. You may discover in the course of your keyword analysis that your SEO opportunity is large. For example, Mint.com learned early on that while many, many, many (millions of) people were searching for money management advice, the sites that were trying to SEO that term were not executing effectively. Mint went all in on winning that set of terms, featuring an extensive, active blog on money management. When Mint won their key terms, they were able to drive millions of visitors per month to their site.

If you are one of the rare cases where you realize that you have identified a huge traffic niche that is being poorly managed by the status quo, don't hesitate to go all-in. SEO is a lucrative and productive traffic builder over time. There is no other way to see 30%+ click-through rates, particularly where the marginal cost of acquiring that traffic is zero.

If you are going all-in on SEO, you should buy some more books, sign up for SEOMoz, etc.. Having said that, I want to give you the 20% of tips that will help you realize 80% of the value.

By and large, Google is very good. They do a good job of recognizing that content is topical, popular, and appropriate to a search term. The need to build link farms has declined significantly with the last few updates of Google de-emphasizing page rank in their algorithms. Hence, building strong relationships with people linking to your content is not as important as it was a few years ago (although if it happens, it is absolute magic and allows you to completely own a set of terms). The first place to start is architecting your own site and your link structure.

Just as search engines need to be able to read the page in order to understand what the page is about, they also need to see links in order to find the content. A crawl-able link structure, i.e. one that lets their spiders (the name for Google's robots that traverse the web (get it? spiders?)) browse the pathways of a website, is critical to ensure that the search engine sees and appreciates the value of the content you are creating. Too many sites make the mistake of structuring their navigation in ways that search engines cannot access, impacting their ability to get pages listed in the search engines' indices.

There are things you should do on the page in the HTML. The goal is for spiders to think your page is about that specific keyword. That means using that keyword. But don't go overboard. Ever seen a page like this: "Ann's cheap San Diego flower shop is the best cheap San Diego flower shop for all your flower needs.

Contact a cheap San Diego flower shop easily and get flowers from the San Diego flower shop of Ann."

Another lame trick that people used to try was to put all that text on the page in the exact same color as the page background, effectively hiding this lameness. Now Google and other spiders detect that the text is the same color as the page background and severely penalize them.

Let's call that "trying too hard". They are trying to rank for a term and have bought into the persistent SEO myth that keyword density, a mathematical formula that divides the number of words on a page by the number of instances of a given keyword, is used by the search engines for ranking calculations.

It is important that you use the exact phrase that you are trying to rank for in your copy, but don't bother going crazy like that. It is better to be seen as a credible source linked to by third parties than spam the Google search engine, which generally does not value this. Use keywords intelligently and with usability in mind.

Use the keyword in the title tag at least once. Try to keep the keyword as close to the beginning of the title tag as possible. Try to mention your target keyword just once prominently near the top of the page, then another one or two times, including variations, in the body copy on the page – sometimes a few more if there's a lot of text content.

Think about the "alt" attributes of an image on the page. (This is the textual description associated with an image for readers that are blind or are using a browser that does not display images.) This not only helps with web search, but also image search, which can occasionally bring valuable traffic.

Finally, think about the meta description tag. While this data is not used by the search engines for ranking the page, it is displayed to searchers as an abstract of the page. This is a very strong chance to shape your marketing message around this keyword.

Beyond the HTML and navigation, the URL scheme matters as well. By this, I mean that a URL that looks like this: "www.cheaprealestate.com/cheap-real-estate.html" will tend to be viewed by Google as being more about cheap real estate than a URL like "www.testsite.com/123abc.html", all other things being equal. In fact, even if all things are not completely equal, URL structure is viewed by Google as a powerful indicator of relevancy. It is important to structure the site to exploit this fact.

Place yourself in the mind of a potential searcher and look at your URL. If it is easy to predict the content on the page, then the URL is appropriately descriptive.

If your page is targeting a specific term or phrase, make sure to include it in the URL. However, do not try to stuff in multiple keywords for SEO purposes. Overuse of keywords will result in less usable URLs and can trip spam filters.

If you are feeling technically bent, you can go a step further and simplify URLs even more. The best URLs are human readable without lots of parameters, numbers and symbols. Using technologies like mod_rewrite you can dynamically convert even a strong URL like "www.cheaprealestate.com/cheap-real-estate.html" into a more effective URL like "www.cheaprealestate.com/cheap-real-estate". (#Protip: Some search engines struggle to consume a space or an underscore in a URL. Use hyphens between words. That is the standard.)

Finally, speed matters. Google considers the speed a page loads at as a factor in its rankings. If your page does not load quickly, it will be penalized. But let's be clear about what this means because if you spend a few minutes Googling, you will find a lot of people talking about this. In the only study that I am aware of on the subject, the correlation they found was not to total page load time, but "time-to-first-byte".[4] This is an interesting tradeoff. They did not want to penalize people that had a lot of content or a complex layout – that might be penalizing the best sites on the Internet or the sites with the most comprehensive answers to a given query. Instead, they penalize sites that are simply slow to begin responding.

There are not a lot of things that someone can do about this in a lean way. The answer would seem to imply that taking advantage of high speed content distribution networks (CDNs) like Amazon Web Services to distribute your site around the world would be the best strategy to ensure that your site begins returning content quickly. Alternately, making sure that things like large database queries do not delay the beginning of content being returned to browsers seems valuable. Given that total page load time do not affect results, you should not over invest in this area, at least in regards to SEO.

Generally speaking, faster page loads are great. Google and others have done studies that indicate that faster page load times correlate with higher conversion rates. Shopzilla decreased their page load time by five seconds and saw a 7%-12% increase in conversion rates[5]. Amazon reported in 2006 that every 100ms in page load improvement drove 1% increases in revenue.

Last, people talk about page rank – the process of getting links to your site to demonstrate your sites credibility. This is important, but it is something that best happens organically. The time it takes to finesse link acquisition puts it in the 80% of extra work that delivers marginal incremental value. Some people will suggest link farming or buying links. Don't buy links. Just don't. Google is better at detecting them than you are at hiding them. #truth.

To summarize:

- Crawlable link structure
- Term near beginning of title tag
- Term near beginning of article, one or two other times
- Alt image names
- Meta descriptions
- Readable URL with hyphens
- Maybe accelerate first bit return?

Content Marketing

Content marketing is as popular as growth hacking. Interest in content marketing is a self-fulfilling prophecy: Generating content that is popular is the essence of content marketing. By the act of the creation of popular content, content marketing self-markets its own value. When you see good content and you envy it, that is the marketing of content marketing!

The result is that everyone wishes that they were making great content, be it infographics, long form articles, popular slideshows on Slideshare or viral videos.

A lot of people talk about content marketing like it is the holy grail of advertising. It is good marketing. Let's put it in context. Content marketing consists of three steps. The first step is producing great content. The second step is creating awareness of that content. The third step is the long term SEO benefit of the content creation.

Creating great content is hard, but frankly, great content is a dime a dozen. Making great content is not dissimilar from making a great product. What distinguishes much of this content is the marketing of that content. This marketing is, in many ways, no different than other marketing activities except that it is difficult to systematize in a way that guarantees success. Trying to gain traction for your content marketing is a grind-it-out business that is fundamental PR and marketing.

If you are going to create content, you think about it the same way that you think about other aspects of your SEO work: Think about the third step - the creation of long term SEO value. Pick a keyword or term that you can win by creating a great piece of content marketing for it, then market the heck out of it to create inbound links.

For certain kinds of information-heavy products, content marketing can be extremely effective, but because it can be structurally difficult to test and optimize content marketing due to its hit driven nature, for many businesses, content marketing may be a red herring.

Last tip: Many people think about breaking things into a variety of sub-domains. Like your blog is at blog.mycompany.com and your career page is at careers.mycompany.com. Sometimes that is a technical necessity. Maybe you are using something like tumblr for your blog and it is difficult to make it part of an existing sub-domain. While Google says that it doesn't matter if you create a sub-domain or a directory off the main domain, history has shown that keeping everything in the main domain results in far better SEO outcomes.

Measuring SEO Winning

Search Engine Share of Referring Visits

Every month, it's critical to keep track of the contribution of each traffic source for your site. Google Analytics generally breaks these into a few buckets:

- **Direct Navigation:** This is people putting your URL in their browser. This is a really important metric that we will devote a section to shortly. Initially, this number will be super small.
- **Referral Traffic:** This comes from your advertising campaigns or people linking to you.
- **Search Traffic:** Traffic from a search engine. This is quite germane given the subject at hand.

Your search engine traffic should be high as a percentage of your overall traffic, particularly if you are not doing a lot of advertising. When you get started with SEO, it will typically be south of 20% of your traffic. It needs to be 60%+. If it is 60% and stable, even as your other traffic is growing, that reflects your growth in the minds of the search engines as a reputable place to send customers. It might decrease as you ramp paid marketing efforts, but you would like paid marketing efforts to be having a secondary effect of creating positive SEO juice. As you ramp up the business and marketing activity and achieve product/market fit, you should be slowly ramping up SEO commensurately. Some of this SEO work will be work you do. Some will be SEO benefits that naturally accrue as word of your goods and services spread, your brand

and traffic improve and you business grows, establishing the authority of your message in the machine brains of search engines. As you are able to grow your business into tackling more competitive terms, your ability to win those terms by leveraging your brand, your traffic, and your marketing capability will grow hand in hand with your business.

Visits Referred by Specific Search Engines Terms and Phrases

Understanding the keywords that send you traffic is the essence of your SEO strategy. If you don't know the answer to this question, then you aren't really playing the game. You'll want to keep track of these on a regular basis to help identify new trends in keyword demand, gauge your performance on key terms and find terms that are bringing significant traffic that you're potentially under optimizing.

An important aspect of this is to track branded and unbranded terms. In the context of SEO success, we want to carve out and disregard all of the searches for your company. For example, to re-use the Cogmap example, when people search for "Cogmap" and click the "Cogmap" link, that is not particularly important in this context. You don't get credit for that because your companies name is a very low volume search term. And ranking first for your own brand name is fairly easy. If they search for "org chart wiki" and click the "Cogmap" link, that is a victory for the power of SEO.

This is useful in other contexts, as we shall discuss, but if you are measuring your SEO might, it is a red herring.

Conversion Rate by Search Term Query/Phrase

Setting up a constant cycle of analytics around the LTV of customers for every search term is very important. Initially, your data will be so sparse that it will take long periods of time to provide enough results to truly understand activity. Further, even as traffic grows, you will frequently learn that "long tail" terms are some of the most valuable and best performing terms. For example, if someone searches for "jacket", that might indicate that they are fairly high in the funnel, whereas if they search for "blue North Face jacket", that might indicate that they are much closer to actually converting at the bottom of the funnel. While terms like this might have limited volume, they can be so effective that they are worth monitoring.

If you find that your conversion rate is extremely high for a term, you should check where you rank for those terms. If you don't rank first, it might be worth making an SEO investment in this area. Moving from fifth position to first position will give you ten times as much traffic.

Just sayin'.

When it comes to the bottom line for your organization, no metric matter as much as conversion rate.

Number of Pages Receiving at Least One Visit from Search Engines

Google Webmaster Tools can help you understand the total number of pages that have been indexed by the Google search engine. Beyond this, it is productive to understand how many pages are actually seeing search engine traffic. As you work on each aspect of your SEO plan and become increasingly sophisticated, the trend line should rise, showing that more and more pages are earning their way into the engines' results. Pages receiving search traffic is a very instructive long tail metric.

This is important because while it is great to know that Google is aware of your content, it is a completely different value proposition to know that a page has successfully ranked for a term and attracted a click. This is the gold standard for building your credibility as a brand in the mind of the Google machine.

Navigational Queries as KPI

One other metric that is interesting in the context of Google Analytics and organic search is direct navigational queries in Google. We mentioned that these searches for branded terms are not useful as a gauge of SEO effectiveness, but direct navigational queries are a powerful tool to tell you how strongly you are impacting a market. When trying to find a web site, many people simply go to Google and type in the domain. When the domain comes up as the first search result, they click it and go.

This predilection is essentially a strong vanity metric to understand how effectively you are achieving "awareness" in the market. To the extent that PR is very difficult to measure and causes spikes and troughs in traffic, looking at navigational queries is a valuable tool for smoothing this data out.

The easiest way to look at this is to use Google Trends. Here is a Google Trends report for "Instagram".

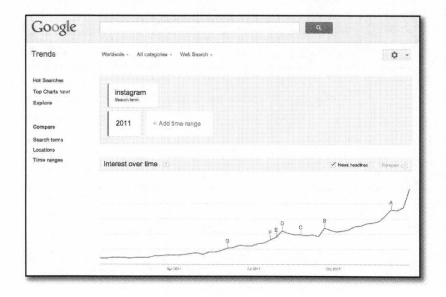

This is a strong, healthy brand. You can see how, over the course of 2011, there are more and more people simply typing "Instagram" into the Google search engine bar.

Here is Snapchat from 2012 to the beginning of 2014:

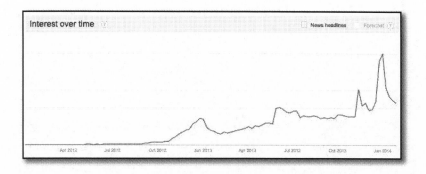

You can see the spikes driven by news events. Once again, there is a powerful upward trend demonstrating that this product has strong brand momentum.

If this graph were flat or declining, it would indicate a serious problem, in spite of whatever PR results, paid customer acquisition, and SEO effectiveness you may be yielding. Direct navigational queries are an unfiltered source of consumer demand. If consumers are looking for you, direct navigational queries will appear.

Of course, if you do something big, you will see a spike, but if the spike does not continue to build over time, you will be able to recognize the unsustainable nature of the activity from a brand value perspective.

This is a valuable metric for measuring the overall effectiveness of your marketing and for that reason is a good number to track over time. Unfortunately, the value of this metric is its longitudinal nature. It is not a number that can be looked at in the short term. It tells you if you need to work harder, but it doesn't tell you if what you just did worked. Hence it is primarily a vanity metric by nature.

Notes

1. http://www.kalzumeus.com/2010/01/24/startup-seo/
2. http://searchenginewatch.com/article/2345638/PPC-Click-Through-Rate-by-Position-Does-Rank-Matter-Data
3. http://www.mecmanchester.co.uk/blog/evaluating-the-uk-search-marketing-landscape-infographic/
4. http://moz.com/blog/how-website-speed-actually-impacts-search-ranking
5. http://cdn.oreillystatic.com/en/assets/1/event/29/Shopzilla_s%20

Site%20Redo%20-
%20You%20Get%20What%20You%20Measure%20Presentation.p
pt

CHAPTER 10

Growth by People: Virality

Growth Hacking is a very in-vogue thing to talk about. Many start-ups say growth hacking is their strategy for gaining new customers with minimal expense. They say this because it is the in-vogue thing to say. And Growth Hacking is great. Let's be clear: Growth Hacking is something the world needs more of.

The concept of growth hacking came from Facebook's "growth team" – an engineering team dedicated to projects prioritized not by long term revenue value or organizational priorities, but strictly focused on things that helped Facebook acquire additional consumers as quickly as possible. Things like integrations with partners tended to be handled by the growth team. Where at other companies, a partner integration might have taken a month or more just to schedule and prioritize in the business, if Facebook saw an opportunity to add a substantial number of customers, that opportunity would be funneled to the growth team, where an engineer could start work on it right away.

Growth hacking sprang from an acknowledgement that large parts of customer acquisition in a technology business come not from traditional marketing activities, but from underlying technology and engineering work. Growth hacking as a term people throw around has probably jumped the shark, but we recognize that in the big scheme of things, there are three kinds of tools for driving traffic:

Organic: Things that can be done to the site that make people choose to come to your site more frequently. SEO to make Google direct more searchers to your site is one of the most popular forms of organic traffic improvements one can make. A more nefarious example of an organic growth strategy was when the Path app launched for iPhones, it would surreptitiously scrape all of the user's contacts from their address book and contact them on the user's behalf to drive sign ups. This is using technology to create viral growth, but not necessarily by making a great product.

Strategic Partnerships/Integrations: This can include things like APIs that integrate with third parties. For example, Photobucket built their business by integrating with MySpace and being the easiest way to share photos in that large social network. Zynga marketed their products through a deep technical integration with Facebooks APIs. Further, Zynga and similar companies, many in the mobile space, built out cross-promotional marketing technology to drive consumers that engaged in one of their products into a broad range of their offerings.

Paid Marketing: Growth hackers don't play here, but their skill sets do. This is about creating a sustained marketing velocity. Growth hacking has limits, for example, there are only so many strategic technical integrations that can be invested in with strong traffic returns. Also, they typically require that another party express interest. This is easy for someone like Facebook where many third parties have interest. For most start-ups, attracting strong partners is very difficult. Paid marketing is bounded only by your efficiency, your capital and the LCV of the product you are marketing. This is great because as a start-up, if you are relying on a third party to ensure the success of your business, you are taking a terrible, unmanageable risk.

K Factor

Your product and conversion path is now optimized, so when someone comes to your site, the odds of them becoming a customer are high, but that is not enough. To maximize your opportunity, you need to think about generating referrals and viral mechanics to be successful.

Viral mechanics are something to consider but they may not be an area of focus for you early on. If your business doesn't have a viral mechanic at its core, optimizing a bolt-on function may not be a good investment. As we said earlier, retention and stickiness is a more important aspect of demonstrating product/market fit and showing that customers are getting value from the product.

If you want to be a hipster on the Internet today, you have to talk about your "K factor". K factor is a term borrowed from medicine to talk about how viral something is. Essentially, in medicine, they talk about two things: The rate of distribution of the disease and how likely someone it contacts becomes infected. The product of these two percentages is the diseases K factor. If the K factor is equal to 1, then the disease is in a steady state, neither growing nor shrinking. If it exceeds 1, then the disease is spreading at an exponential rate. If it is less than 1, than it shrinks at an exponential rate.

This can be translated into digital marketing by considering the following formula:

R = number of referrals sent by each customer

CVR = percent of referrals that turn into customers

K = R * CVR

So, the way the theory works, if R were two and CVR was 100%, then every customer would refer two people that became customers and the business would be a super-powered flywheel, with a single customer creating a wave of future customers where the incremental CPA was zero.

Of course, that doesn't take into account viral cycle time – an equally important variable. Further, this doesn't account for the complexity of customer churn and market size, but the additional mathematical rigor offered by using a more complex formula doesn't yield a more actionable outcome.

Viral Cycle Time

Viral cycle time is a measure of how long it takes the viral loop to occur. In our earlier example, we indicated that each customer would refer two future people to become customers. If it takes a year for that to take place, it is ok, but it is unlikely that the business will experience truly dramatic growth. If it takes a day, then amazing things can happen.

Let's look at viral cycle times impact on growth given these variables:

R = 2

CVR = 100%

K = 2 * 100% = 2.00

	Time				
Cycle Time	0	10	20	30	40
1	1	2,047	2,097,151	2,147,483,650	2,199,023,259,839
2	1	63	2,047	65,535	2,097,151
5	1	7	31	127	511
10	1	3	7	15	31
20	1	2	3	5	7
40	1	1	2	2	3

If it takes 40 days to get those two referrals turned into customers, at the end of 40 days your viral loop will have netted you: three customers. If it takes one day for your viral loop to turn those two referrals turned into customers, then at the end of 40 days you will have more than two billion customers. And that is with the exact same K factor. So the spread is equally likely, it is simply very slow. While some might say, "Any positive K factor means over a sufficiently long enough period of time, I will get two billion customers", few businesses want to wait for it.

If your K factor is 1, a rapid cycle time can still produce exciting outcomes for your business. Let's look at the same table with a different variable mix:

$R = 2$

$CVR = 50\%$

$K = 2 * 50\% = 1.00$

	Time				
Cycle Time	0	10	20	30	40
1	1	11	21	31	41
2	1	6	11	16	21
5	1	3	5	7	9
10	1	2	3	4	5
20	1	1	2	2	3
40	1	1	1	2	2

Here we can see that with a sufficiently accelerated cycle time, even at a K factor of only one we can see strong viral growth. A K factor of 1 with a fast cycle time can be more valuable than a 2.00 K factor with a slow cycle time.

Finally, consider a situation where K is less than 1. When K is close to zero, no one refers anyone and the referrals that do take place are ineffective, then there is basically no benefit due to virality. However, if the K factor is close to one, the results are more interesting.

R = 2

CVR = 40%

K = 2 * 40% = 0.80

	Time				
Cycle Time	0	10	20	30	40
1	1	5	5	5	5
2	1	4	5	5	5
5	1	2	3	4	4
10	1	2	2	3	3
20	1	1	2	2	2
40	1	1	1	2	2

For short cycle times, it is apparent how the low K factor impedes growth of the product. For long cycle times, there is almost no change. In fact, there is almost no change from when the K factor was 2.00. There are two takeaways hiding here: first, for long cycle times, it almost doesn't matter what the K factor is. There is no benefit to the business if it takes a long time to generate the viral activity. Second, if the K factor is high, but not 1.00, there is still substantial benefit. For every person that you sign up, it drives over a relatively short time five more sign-ups. It isn't exponential growth, but the value of four customer acquisitions is not insubstantial, particularly when the cost of acquisition is negligible.

So when thinking of customer acquisition, K is the multiplier, but it is lifted exponentially by cycle time. Hence cycle time can be much more impactful than improving your viral coefficient.

Viral Marketing

To build out our viral referral engine, we need something that people use to reach out quickly and often. Something that people will perceive as being valuable and act on quickly. We can break these into several different buckets.

The first is sharing mechanisms. Typically, things that attract sharing are things that people find valuable. This could include applications, data, news content, and things with monetary value such as coupons. Additionally, people share things they find entertaining. This could be something funny, something amazing in the news, or a casual game. In a study of New York Times content sharing habits, researchers observed that people preferred to share positive messages, long form content, and things that provoked an emotional response.[1]

Another strategy is to build sharing into the use of the product. Things like email, Skype, and social networks are examples of how a mechanism like this works. Cogmap, the organization chart wiki, offers private maps that people build and then share. Without sharing, the maps have dramatically less value to the person building the map. A simpler example is Hotmail, which added a marketing message about Hotmail to the end of every email message a consumer sent. Suddenly every email message became a marketing message consumers shared to spread the Hotmail word.

An even more powerful mechanic is one that rewards the initiator for completing the viral loop. Groupon provides an excellent example of this approach, offering a discount to the sharer when the sharee takes advantage of the shared offer.[9]

When Aloha launched, they gave each person who signed up "pre-launch" a referrer link. When people used the referrer link to

---

9. I am quite sure "sharee" is the technical term for this person. And I am trademarking it.

subsequently sign up, Aloha credited the initial person with free products.

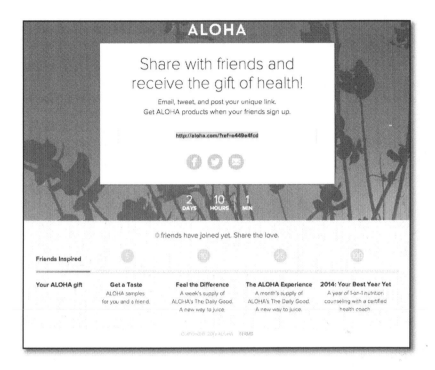

Candy Crush, the popular iPhone game, allows players to get extra lives by involving their friends in the game. Integration into the Facebook social graph allows the game to engage players by letting them ask for more lives, unlock more levels, and compare their scores to their friends all via integration with Facebook.

Identifying the best mechanisms for viral mechanics around your experience and optimizing those mechanics can increase K factor, decrease viral cycle time and create incremental value for the organization.

While throwing around your K factor makes you sound like a Silicon Valley hipster, from a measurement perspective, you need to measure the time it takes to move a person from activation to referral, the number of referrals they make, and the acceptance rate of those referrals. That informs the strength of your call to action which is a key driver of your K factor.

Between conversion rate optimization, optimizing referrals and the core viral loop, this rounds out the work we have on the experience people have on the site/app/product. Up until this point, the objective for acquisition has been to only get enough traffic to provide us with data to optimize the experience. Now that we have completed this work, we are ready to start trying to drive real traffic to the site.

Notes

1.
http://www.nytimes.com/2010/02/09/science/09tier.html?_r=0

CHAPTER 11

Growth by Cash: Paid Acquisition

Ready For Banners!

Display Advertising

Desktop display advertising is what someone means when you think of most online advertising. You are on your computer, visiting a web site, and you see an advertisement on it. The IAB (Internet Advertising Bureau, the industries self-regulating body) has defined a variety of standard formats for banners displayed within a web page.[1]

Banners are inexpensive and they are everywhere. The result is, as we scale up revenue, you will probably need to buy some. Many of these salespeople managing performance ad products will be looking for ways to screen you out as being "too small" for them. The better you speak the language, the more easily you will be able to insinuate yourself into the industry and understand how apples and oranges compare to each other.

When people in the industry talk about ad formats and sizes, they use a colloquial of pixel dimensions (width x height) to describe the creative ad unit. Standard formats include:

- 728x90 ad units (sometimes called "leaderboards"). This is 728 pixels wide and 90 pixels tall.

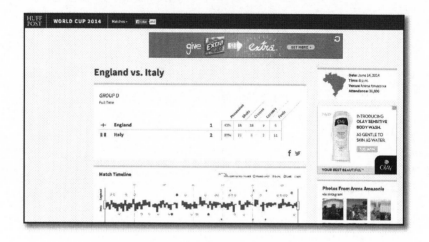

- 300x250 ad units (sometimes called a "Medium Rectangle")

- 160x600 ad units (sometimes called "wide skyscraper")
- 180x150 ad units (sometimes called "rectangles")

There have been other ad units historically, for example 468x60 and 640x80 ad units were popular when computers were older and screens were smaller, as was a 120x600 ad unit (the original "skyscraper"), but over time these units have virtually disappeared.

As advertisers have tended to demand larger units and as large units tend to perform better (resulting in higher CPM payouts by ad networks), publishers have tended toward the larger units. Further, for ad networks and ad agencies there is a tipping point where it is not worth developing assets for a size where they are not running many impressions, meaning that those impressions become unsaleable for a publisher. The result has been that as critical mass on larger units is reached, demand for smaller units evaporates overnight.

Even larger ad units are coming as part of the IAB's "Rising Stars" initiative, the 970x250 "Billboard", the 300x600 filmstrip, and the 300x1050 "Portrait" will cover most of your screen in ads if advertisers have anything to say about it.[2] (And they do!) Here the New York Times is running the new Billboard ad:

These ad units are so intrusive and large, they have been very slow to roll out to publishers, but increasingly dense monitors that pack more and more pixels into the screen will inevitably lead us down the road to these larger units.[10] The industry has seen a

---

10. Although the increasing density of screens will make each pixel smaller, compensating significantly for this fact. When 728x90s were first released, it seemed like they covered half the screen, but with most monitors at a 1028 or higher pixel density, 728 pixels suddenly seems very small. Expect this trend to continue but publisher will always make sure that these intrusive units don't appear until many of their consumers user experiences are not negatively impacted.

steady decline in click-through rates (CTR), with the average banner yielding a less than 0.1% CTR (one click for every 1000 ads
displayed - a decline from over 1% in the early days of banners).[3]
More impactful units are a reaction to this trend.

Banner ads have changed significantly over the last decade.
Originally, banner ads were simple graphical images. Today ,
many banner ads use rich media to incorporate video, audio, ani-
mations, buttons, forms, or other interactive elements using
HTML5. During the intervening period, the industry built banner
ads using java and flash, but those have been largely deprecated in
favor of HTML5.

Similarly, pop-up and pop-under ads, which displayed a new
brower window that opened above or under a web site visitors
initial browser window were very popular for a brief period of
time (due to phenomenal performance for advertisers), but the
negative impact on publisher user experience was so dramatic that
they have largely disappeared. Further, the negative consumer experience led to many modern browsers implementing tools to
block these kinds of ads. These have been replaced by things like
overlay ads, a type of rich media advertisement that appears super-
imposed over the requested website's content.[11]

A similar technology that was once widespread was the installation of toolbars. Many of these toolbar products generated revenue by hijacking ad slots. They would identify ads on a page, then
traffic their own Google ads to make money. This kind of arbi-

---

11. In an effort to not become overly academic, I will now proceed to skip past a
host of notes about creative issues. Things like expanding ads, interstitial ad
units, and even things like "trick banners", where the advertiser shows an error
message or chat message that attempts to induce a user click unrelated to a
compelling advertiser message.

trage was detrimental to both advertisers and consumers and has largely disappeared.

You will want the most intrusive ad units you can get, but generally, if you are able to buy on a performance basis, you should be indifferent. If you are only paying for an ad when someone clicks and places an order on your site, if the people you are working with want to run very, very tiny ads, then the only risk is that they are wasting your time with their bad ideas.

Display advertising is extraordinarily lucrative. Internet advertising revenues hit historic highs nearly every quarter today. In the fourth quarter of 2012, they exceeded $10 billion for the first time.[4] And it is expected to continue growing by 19% year over year for the next several years.[5]

Annual revenue 2003-2012 ($ billions)

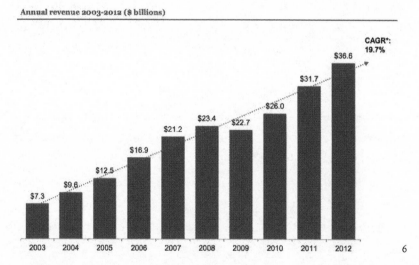

Online display advertising is dominated by the top five biggest players in the industry: Google, AOL, Microsoft, Yahoo! and Facebook. Collectively these five companies accounted for 53.8% of total display ad revenue in 2011.[7] While the dominant players are all household names, the size of each of their piece of the pie has changed in the past few years and it is expected to change even more.

eMarketer.com projects that Google will displace Facebook as the biggest seller of desktop display ads in 2013, and they are expected to grow their lead in the future.[8] Whether these predictions come true or not remains to be seen, but the current top five stand to control a huge share of the online advertising dollars for a long time to come.

Every one of these publishers offers inventory that historically performs extraordinarily well. Unfortunately, the demand for their inventory mirrors their effectiveness. If you start to invest dollars in display advertising, these brands will contact you. It is important that you recognize that these are the big guys. They need ten million dollars from you for you to really get their attention. There are probably not great values here. Tread carefully.

Video

Video advertising is very appealing to advertisers, who have grown up on a steady diet of television advertising. They are already developing 15 and 30 second spots to run on television, creatives that have cost, in some cases, hundreds of thousands of dollars. The ability to leverage these creatives into a new medium is valuable to them. Further, these creatives are compelling: TV advertisements generally tell a story. They are extremely effective at achieving an emotional connection with consumers.

As video consumption on the Internet has sky-rocketed, so has the opportunity for advertising with video.

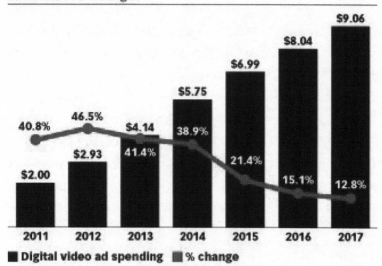

US Digital Video Ad Spending, 2011-2017
billions and % change

Note: includes advertising that appears on desktop and laptop computers as well as mobile phones and tablets; data through 2011 is derived from IAB/PwC data; includes in-banner, in-stream (such as pre-roll and overlays) and in-text (ads delivered when users mouse-over relevant words)
Source: eMarketer, March 2013

156262   www.eMarketer.com⁹

Video advertising is in great demand because television advertising is so extraordinarily effective and is something that clients are comfortable with. For agencies recommending it to clients, it is an easy sell. I was recently talking with a very large ad agency and they described the video advertising opportunity as a money give-away. They would "make it rain" (their words) for anyone with pre-roll inventory on quality content.

For you, the opportunity of video advertising is less clear. Unless you have the ability to produce high quality video, this opportunity is probably not for you. Furthermore, very little video inventory is sold on a true performance basis - although at Youtube, they only charge you if someone actually watches the entire video. There is so much demand for video inventory that publishers here are less inclined to create opportunities for startup advertisers to be successful. Regardless, you should know the lingo because it could be very effective and I expect that as supply grows, performance opportunities will present themselves.

When people talk about video advertising, they inevitably throw around two important acronyms, VAST and VPAID.

VAST is a simple script for the video ad. VAST just provides consistent instructions to the video player on how to handle an ad. It tells the video player what the ad should do; how it should show up in the player, how long it should display, whether or not it is skippable, where to find the ad (i.e. the ad server), and what the click-through url should be.

VPAID addresses the next step in engaging consumers: While it is easy for advertisers to simply show a TV spot that they had previously created in a pre-roll video slot, making the ads interactive is where they want to take creatives. VAST supports in-stream video ad formats. VPAID allows compliant video players to display rich interactive media ads. VPAID builds upon VAST to enable rich ad experiences, and enhanced viewer analytics.

Before VAST, there was not a common in-stream advertising protocol for video players, which made scalable distribution of ads impossible. In order to serve ads to multiple publishers using disparate proprietary video players, ad--serving organizations had to develop slightly different ad responses for every publisher/video player targeted. VAST provides a common protocol that enables ad servers to use a single ad response format across multiple publishers/video players.

Youtube now has more than one billion unique users per month, so in that respect it demonstrates the appeal of video advertising, but video's relationship to TV leads to a pricing structure unfavorable to early stage DR-based pricing. Even Google prices Youtube on a cost per view, demonstrating performance by only charging people for video ads that are viewed for at least 30 seconds.

Unfortunately, while that is powerful branding, I suspect that this pricing model will make it impractical for us to apply our direct response strategies and expect reasonable backend price-to-performance ratios.

Mobile

Mobile advertising is not dissimilar from traditional display advertising – except that it is on a mobile device! There are a number of dimensions in which mobile advertising offers the promise of being interesting and relevant, but the most important thing to say up front about mobile is that click-through rates are high. Today, they are frequently higher than 0.4%. That is quadruple the average desktop display campaign. And in my experience, they achieve this performance while still showing similar back-end conversion metrics to desktop or video advertising. Of course, the back-end metrics I have looked at are generally relevant to the context of such an ad: They are great for physical retail and casual gaming advertising. I have little experience using them for more traditional commerce sites, although anecdotal evidence implies that it is impactful here as well. If you are a retail establishment, mobile app or game, or another tool where mobile is relevant, this is must-try advertising for growing your business.

There are two kinds of popular mobile ad units: A banner across the page (The IAB standard is 320x50) and an interstitial ad unit which covers the entire screen. There are also tablet ad units which are tending towards 728x90 and 300x250 desktop display formats because they are formats that advertisers are accustomed to working with already.

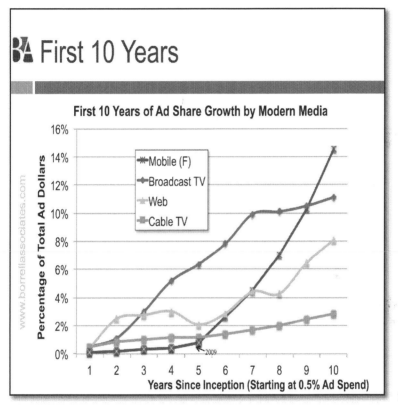

Mobile advertising is a market expected to grow very quickly – Zenith Optimedia forecasts that mobile advertising will grow by an average of 50% a year between 2013 and 2016[11], driven by the rapid adoption of smartphones and tablets. By 2016, the size of the mobile market will have tripled.[12]

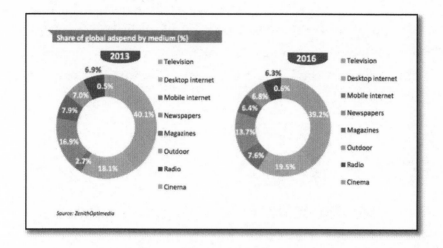

Display advertising has been around for more than a decade. Mobile is just starting. From a market size perspective, digital advertising was around the same size as mobile is today way back in 2005.[13]

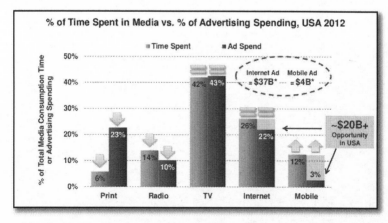

14

All of these meta-trends lead to one inevitable conclusion: As people shift their computing and consumption patterns to mobile devices and tablets, ad spend will inevitably follow. The result is that groups like eMarketer expect mobile advertising to grow larger than desktop advertising in just a few years.

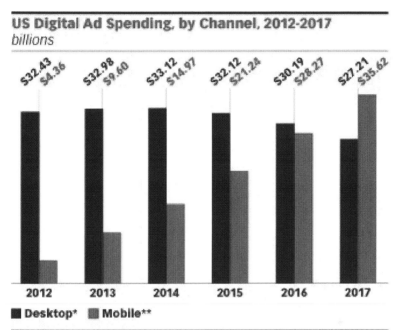

US Digital Ad Spending, by Channel, 2012-2017
billions

	2012	2013	2014	2015	2016	2017
Desktop*	$32.43	$32.98	$33.12	$32.12	$30.19	$27.21
Mobile**	$4.36	$9.60	$14.97	$21.24	$28.27	$35.62

■ **Desktop*** ■ **Mobile****

Note: *includes spending primarily on desktop-based ads; **includes classified, display (banners and other, rich media and video), email, lead generation, messaging-based and search advertising; ad spending on tablets is included
Source: eMarketer, Dec 2013

166074   www.eMarketer.com [15]

One of the areas where people expect much of that growth to occur is in hyperlocal targeting and local advertising. Many advertisers that had few reasons to market online suddenly have a powerful ROI for marketing if they are reaching people engaged in nearby communities. The classic example here is reaching people with a Starbucks coupon as they are walking by the Starbucks. BIA/Kelsey predicts that mobile local advertising will outpace mobile national advertising by 2016 as mobile advertising grows to more than $9 billion.[16]

The nature of mobile has an impact on how advertisers think about digital marketing. Phones are personal devices – every person has their own, never sharing – and they are with you at all times as you move around. The concept that there is now a one to one relationship between people and the devices that receive advertising implies a powerful tool for connecting advertising to relevant consumers.

The growth of mobile devices and their cousin the tablet are changing computing. Tablet advertising is typically thought of as part of the the mobile ecosystem because they share an operating system and set of applications. Even developers think of them as all part of one ecosystem.

Affiliate

Many describe affiliate advertising as the dark underbelly of the Internet.

Affiliate marketing (sometimes called lead generation) occurs when advertisers organize third parties to generate potential customers for them. Third-party affiliates receive payment based on sales generated through their promotion of products and services.

The most well-known example is Amazon. Almost anyone can sign up as an Amazon affiliate. When you are an Amazon affiliate, you can pick any product that you want to "sell" on behalf of Amazon and Amazon will provide you with a customized URL that encodes your "affiliate" ID into it. When someone clicks on that URL, they are transported to the Amazon site and shown the product you selected. Amazon also captures your ID and knows that you sent that customer to them. If the consumer subsequently buys that product then you receive a cut. So Amazon (and other affiliate organizers) use affiliates as an ultimate bottom-of-the-funnel revenue generator. They don't care how you do it, they only care that you sell their products.

This is almost certainly not the advertising for you, but studying affiliate techniques is a lesson in the most powerful tools one can use for generating conversions online. While it is unlikely that you will be able to engage affiliates on your behalf, the spirit of the affiliate, if not the dark underbelly, is one worthy of study.

Why is this the dark underbelly? Well, a far less loved, but extremely common example of affiliate marketing is the "flog" (fake blogs), facebook ads marketing affiliate products, and generally shady mechanisms to maximize the sale of ineffective products. You have probably seen ads like this:

That is as affiliate as it gets. This link takes you to a fake blog ("flog") that attempts to sell you a variety of products for which the owner of the flog is paid an affiliate fee.

If you ever wondered, "Are sites like this real?" Nope. They are really, really fake. One web site, wafflesatnoon.com, catalogued a list of all of the names that were used associated with fake pictures of people who lost weight on diet sites. One single set of pictures was used on blogs with more than a dozen different names.

weight-loss-ripoff-photos4

Is this "Ann Conrad", or "Melanie Thomas", or "Kelly Jacobs"?

The Atlantic recently reported on Jesse Willms[17], a leading black hat (criminal or near criminal, as opposed to white hat) affiliate product seller, and described how he offered $80 to affiliate marketers for leads for products that cost far less, then used the customers signed up by affiliate marketers to surreptitiously bill them for dozens of other products. This sort of wide scale shady customer manipulation is detrimental to affiliate marketers businesses, but they flocked to the high payouts offered.

These affiliate advertisers obscure much of the positive work performed by legitimate affiliate advertisers to generate returns for their affiliate partners. Either way, many people consider affiliate advertisers to be some of the smartest advertisers in the industry, with a deep understanding of what makes consumers click and convert and a relentless drive to improve the performance of their campaigns.

In many ways, these affiliate marketers embody the entire set of skills that are discussed in this book.

Email Marketing

Email marketing is one of the most effective types of marketing. While "old-fashioned", it continues to be one of the most effective marketing techniques available to marketers and with the growth of social media and the relationships that marketers have directly with their fan base, the power of email marketing continues to grow.

Everyone uses email. And when people get emails, they frequently open them. That is the power of email marketing. According to the Direct Marketing Association's latest email marketing report (2012[18], 50% of businesses use some sort of Email Service Provider (ESP) system to manage and measure their email efforts and more than 60% indicate that email marketing drives as much revenue as all of their other digital marketing activities combined. On average, email marketing generated $28.50 for every $1 spent on email marketing.

The best kinds of email marketing are bottom-of-the-funnel engagements where advertisers are reaching out to previously engaged customers with one-to-one messages. The worst kinds of email marketing are illegal spam. Randomly emailing email addresses procured from somewhere in the hopes that they will engage with a brand.

Your marketing strategy should have a significant amount of email marketing as a component. We have discussed all the ways email marketing can be used to drive virality and retention, but building a list early in the business lifecycle and using that list to engage and convert customers is incredibly powerful because you control the timing and nature of the engagement.

The most effective email marketers segment their lists into a variety of groups and send them targeted messages depending upon where they are in the product lifecycle. Specific techniques for segmentation that are both common and effective include messages based on:

- Purchase history
- Abandoned shopping carts
- Activating disengaged users

There are many very effective technologies for email marketing that allow businesses to track message effectiveness, user segmentation, and other analytics.

19

One example that combines many of the growth hacking technologies that we have talked about is eBates. eBates is a site that provides discounts on ecommerce purchases to members. When eBates sees a member visit a partner site (via a pixel checking cookies placed on the partner site), it fires off an email to the consumer to remind them to use eBates. This also helps them better understand the kind of products that their consumers are shopping for by analyzing referral data.

Native Ads

Native ads are the "everything else" of the Internet. Notionally, a "native ad" is an advertisement that takes advantage of the sites fundamental purpose to subvert it to advertising in a unique, novel manner.

Promoted Tweets in Twitter, Sponsored Posts in Facebook, and even search marketing for Google are all examples of native advertising formats. The concept of Sponsored Posts would not make sense outside of the Facebook newsfeed.

With these examples, it is easy to understand why the Internet is abuzz with the opportunity of native advertising. The biggest companies on the Internet are using the broad awareness of their platform to offer native advertising experiences to consumers. It makes sense to think that an effective native advertising format will dramatically outperform a standard banner ad placed around the content on the page. Consumers tend to focus on the content in the page; by embedding the advertisement into the content, engagement becomes much more likely.

Unfortunately, most publishers idea of native advertising is a content advertorial, a background image takeover, or some other somewhat random, but not highly engaging format.

Another challenge of native ad formats is that they require extra work by the advertiser to develop. It is likely that without standardization only the largest platforms will be able to justify the creation of native ad formats. Large platforms – such as Twitter and Facebook – have an audience and level of engagement that demands advertiser attention. They are able to make their own rules in many respects. For the rest of the publishers seeking native advertising opportunities, it is hard to convince an agency to justify the investment of crafting a native message for each publisher platform. While standardization would address this by allowing them to leverage native ad creation from one publisher to another, standardization of native ad formats is theoretically an oxymoron. To the extent that they are standard, the odds that they are able to engage consumers in a truly integrated manner are limited.

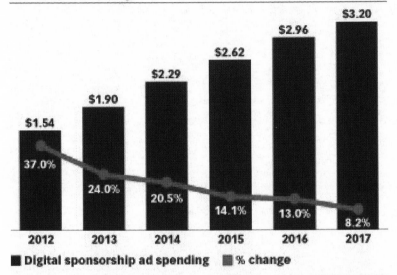

US Digital Sponsorship Ad Spending, 2012-2017
billions and % change

$3.20
$2.96
$2.62
$2.29
$1.90
$1.54

37.0%
24.0%
20.5%
14.1%
13.0%
8.2%

2012   2013   2014   2015   2016   2017

■ Digital sponsorship ad spending   ■ % change

*Note: includes advertising that appears on desktop and laptop computers
as well as mobile phones and tablets*
Source: eMarketer, Dec 2013

166099   www.eMarketer.com

The result is that the market for native advertisements is not expected to be very large in spite of the hype around the market. An eMarketer report in December 2013 framed the growth opportunity as peaking out at a few billion dollars.[20]

There is no question that certain native ads should be a part of any start-ups advertising strategy. Unfortunately for the proponents of native advertising in general, I believe that the investment that is most effective in native ads is around the largest, broadest, and most performance-based platforms you can find. These will be the brand names of the Internet such as Facebook, Google, and Twitter.

The LUMAScape

You know about the different kinds of advertising mechanisms, but there are many different kinds of companies that provide the underlying technology that powers all of these platforms. I mentioned at the beginning of this book the real-time auctions for attention that occur every day. In just the time that it has taken you to read this sentence, literally hundreds of thousands of banners have been dynamically auctioned, scrutinized for the data associated with the consumer, and sold. The good news is that dozens, if not hundreds of companies are working to make those capabilities accessible to your start-up.

In May 2010, Terrence Kawaja, an investment banker at GCA Savvian, was the keynote speaker at the IAB Ad Networks & Exchanges conference. At this conference he presented a Display Advertising Technology Landscape that quickly swept across the industry. This landscape effectively highlighted the component parts of the industry and also spotlit companies that comprised those component parts. It showed the industry in a way that reflected how the industry thought about itself, while providing a built-in marketing opportunity for almost 200 companies.

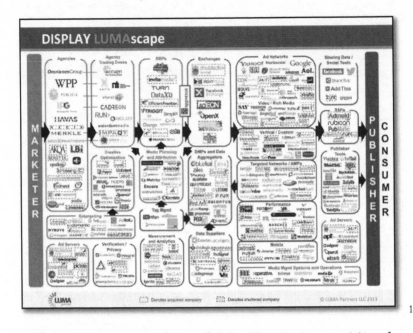

12

From that moment forward, Mr. Kawaja was positioned as a central figure in the industry and was responsible for some of the best-known transactions in the industry, including Invite Media's acquisition by Google. Shortly after that presentation, he left GCA Savvian to start his own investment bank called LUMA Partners and continues to publish LUMAscapes, as they are now known. These LUMAscapes are frequently referenced by corporate development teams when they are beginning to look for potential acquisitions and many start-up CEOs obsess about appearing in the LUMAscapes and their specific position in the diagram.

It also highlighted one of the chief problems of the industry: Too many boxes with too many actors, all fighting over a digital advertising dollar. As ever more intermediaries injected their

12. This is the 2013 version of that slide.
http://www.lumapartners.com/lumascapes/display-ad-tech-lumascape/

business model into the LUMAscape, the value received by publishers as part of a transaction dwindled.

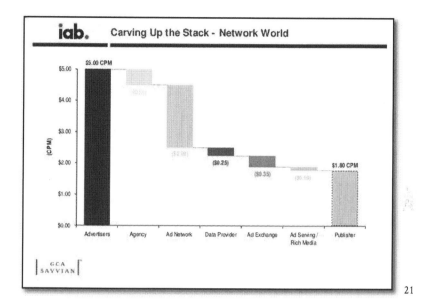

21

This chart illustrates the intermediation taking place. Where an advertiser might pay a $5 CPM for inventory, the agency takes 10%, then the ad network takes 40%, a data provider might charge $0.25 CPMs (more like $1-$2 today), an exchange or SSP might take $0.35 CPMs, and there may be some ad serving fee, third party verification fee, or some other fee ($0.10 up to $2.00). This all comes prior to the publisher getting their payout. Whereas ten years ago, a publisher might have realized 85% to 90% of the value of the $5, now they frequently see less than 40% of the value of the transaction.

Ad Networks

In the advertising industry, publishers are thought of as being easily understood. A publisher's goal is to maximize page views and maximize revenue per page view. Publishers create content that will be of interest to consumers and then attempt to monetize that content as effectively as possible. By understanding their psychology, we will be able to exploit it when we seek to advertise by working with them.

Relatively early on in the life cycle of the Internet, publishers realized the content consumption of material published on the Internet dramatically outpaced their ability to convince advertisers to embrace the Internet. The result was a significant amount of content created by the publisher was not being monetized at all. Publishers could not sell all of the pages they were creating. Savvy publishers realized that tools like Google AdWords could allow them to change this. Suddenly any page view that a publisher could not sell could be "sold" to Google to generate additional marginal revenue and profit. This decision to segment inventory into inventory they sold themselves (termed "premium" or "direct") and inventory remaining that was liquidated through third parties ("remnant") transformed the industry and their business. Displaying Google ads allowed a publisher to employ Google as their de facto extended sales force.

Google AdWords paid on a performance basis. Publishers only receive revenue when they generated a click for the advertiser. The result was an effective RPM, or revenue per page view, that was typically a fraction of the price which the publisher demanded for the page. Publishers had demonstrated that they were willing to risk "the integrity of their rate card" to generate additional revenue. By that, I mean if a publisher was going to market saying that buying a position in their inventory cost $10 CPM, but by bidding for appropriate keyword in Google your ad might appear on the page at an effective CPM (because you're only paying for the click) of four dollars, if advertisers found out then the publisher would risk lost sales at the $10 CPM price as advertisers transition their business to the lower CPM model. In fact, this four dollar CPM is even worse for the publisher because the publisher does not receive the entire four dollars. Google has some margin (today that margin is approximately 32%[22]), that they keep as the middleman of the deal.

Publishers had a difficult choice: risk the integrity of their rate card and take additional marginal revenue from Google or have unsold inventory and risk the integrity of their business. In almost every instance, publishers became comfortable with the risk of doing business with Google. They assuaged their concerns by noting that the businesses were not buying their inventory per se, but rather relevant keywords.

This price differential created an opportunity for newcomers as well. Today we call these companies advertising networks. Advertising networks such as ValueClick, FastClick, and Tribal Fusion looked at the discrepancy between what publishers charge and what they were willing to sell incremental inventory to Google for and saw additional opportunities for disintermediation. The hypothesis was simple: if they were willing to sell inventory to Google for four dollars, they would probably be willing to sell inventory to another company at five dollars. Then all the ad network had to do was identify advertisers willing to pay five dollars for inventory that notionally was worth $10. The only challenge the ad network needed to overcome is getting a publisher comfortable with the concept of the ad network selling their inventory.

The publishers concern generally was whether or not the risk to the integrity of the rate card was so great that it dejustified working with the ad network. The ad networks had to have an argument about both how they differentiated their selling from the publisher and how they protected the integrity of the publishers rate card. The most common argument is that the network sells "blind", meaning that they do not reveal to advertisers the source of the inventory upon which they advertise. An ad network might do this by saying that they work with the five largest sports sites on the Internet, for example. Then the advertiser knows the network is offering high quality inventory while the publisher would feel that the integrity of their rate card was preserved because the advertiser would never know the exact price of the inventory that the publisher had sold to that ad network.

Plus, publishers frequently wanted to work with the advertising network. Consider the below model; the top portion of the model demonstrates publisher revenue if half of their inventory are sold by a third party at a four dollar CPM. A model such as this is not uncommon today. If a new advertising network approaches the publisher and offers to supplant the existing network by paying five dollars CPM then the publisher revenue model looks like the second half of the spreadsheet. With virtually no work, publishers just generated an incremental 7% of additional revenue. For many publishers, finding the most effective advertising networks suddenly became the difference between making aggressive revenue goals in this new digital world and missing revenue goals.

Model 1	Impressions	CPM	Revenue	% of Revenue
Direct Sold	1,000,000	$10.00	$10,000	71%
Remnant	1,000,000	$4.00	$4,000	29%
Total	2,000,000		$14,000	

Model 2	Impressions	CPM	Revenue	% of Revenue
Direct Sold	1,000,000	$10.00	$10,000	67%
Remnant	1,000,000	$5.00	$5,000	33%
Total	2,000,000		$15,000	

It became easy to justify finding ways to work with the most aggressive and most effective advertising networks.

Now publishers were very receptive to the message of advertising networks. The question for advertising was, "given virtually unlimited access to inventory (for inventory far exceed demand), how does one unlock maximum advertising dollars?" Consider this model:

Model 3	Impressions	CPM	Revenue	% of Revenue
Direct Sold	1,000,000	$10.00	$10,000	71%
Network 1	990,000	$4.00	$3,960	28%
Network 2	10,000	$5.00	$50	0.4%
Total	2,000,000		$14,010	

Model 4	Impressions	CPM	Revenue	% of Revenue
Direct Sold	1,000,000	$10.00	$10,000	70%
Network 1	600,000	$4.00	$2,400	17%
Network 2	400,000	$4.50	$1,800	12.7%
Total	2,000,000		$14,200	

In this example, looking at Model Three, Network Two brings an incremental ability for publishers to monetize 10,000 impressions at a five dollars CPM. Unfortunately this generates only $10 in marginal revenue for publisher, potentially not enough to justify publisher investment.

In Model Four, Network Two brings an incremental ability for the publisher to monetize 400,000 impressions at $4.50 CPM. While the absolute value per page for that network is lower, Network Two generates an incremental $200 in revenue, a 1.5% increase.

Further, Network Two just generated $1800 in revenue compared to $50 in revenue in model three. Advertising networks quickly learned that the goal was rarely CPM maximization, but rather exceeding a floor and driving maximum impressions and revenues sold at that price.

Advertising.com

Advertising.com was one of the first and by far the most successful at playing this game. Advertising.com established a unique and novel approach to selling to advertisers. They offered to engage advertisers on a cost per action (CPA) basis. Where most publishers were selling on a cost per page view (CPM), and Google was selling on a cost per click (CPC), Advertising.com was willing to engage advertisers by agreeing only to be paid if the consumer undertook an action as previously defined and agreed to between the advertiser and Advertising.com. These actions may have included things such as interest in refinancing, signing up for an online course, buying a product online, or almost any action that represents a defined, discreetly valuable undertaking to an advertiser.

Consider this: as an advertiser, how much are you willing to pay for a customer? After all this reading, you better be quoting the lifetime value of your customer. Most advertisers were the same way. For example, if an e-commerce site had an average profit margin of 30% and an average transaction size of $100, that site might be willing to pay up to $29.99 for an incremental transaction. If Advertising.com approached the advertiser and suggested that it could find additional customers and charge just 10% of each transaction as its fee-for-service, it would not be unsurprising if the marketing budget to which Advertising.com would be given access to by the marketer was functionally unlimited. Switching sides of the table, the implication is that the amount of revenue Advertising.com could earn from that advertiser was potentially infinite.

By establishing a broad set of these relationships, Advertising.com was able to create a marketplace for impressions unrivaled outside of Google. But how does network monetization actually work?

For any given impression, for any given offer, the effective revenue per page or eRPM is nonzero. Over some horizon, possibly tens of billions of page views, some consumer somewhere could notionally be assumed to do almost anything. Given a set of offers and a set of inventory and some knowledge of the probability that any particular offer has for being successful on a given piece of inventory, it's possible to construct a model that determines for any given inventory the offer that should be displayed to maximize incremental revenue. Given that different offers have different likelihood of success on different inventory, the more offers you have and the more inventory you have, the more likely the compatibility of offers and inventory allowing advertising network to generate significant income for themselves and for publishers.

Many ad networks were started on essentially the same proposition. In many respects, all that an advertising network needs to get started is a hook of some form: magic unicorn blood for targeting, tarot cards that tell us user behavior, or maybe more realistically, "we place anonymous cookies on users we see on the Internet with a high propensity to buy things on sale. Using our network, you can target these 'sale lovers'".

If one were to start an ad network tomorrow, I sometimes joke, if you called twenty ad agencies and told them your hook, they would each give you $10,000 for a test campaign. After all, at some level, these agencies have a fiduciary responsibility to understand how effective your ad network is. If you were to talk to a client and the client called the agency and the agency had never worked with you before, it might reflect poorly on the agency. So you could have $200,000 in revenue fairly quickly. After that, all you have to do is perform. If you don't perform, they don't renew and that is the end of your ad network. In many respects, this led entrepreneurs to believe that ad networks were a sales oriented business. Hundreds of advertising networks, many of them poorly constructed, quickly sprang up. As you grow your marketing, many of these companies will probably call you. You almost certainly do not want to work with them. Even then, people wondered: what could contain the growth of these networks?

Supply Side Platforms

People selling ad inventory proliferated and the result was demands on publishers increased. The result of this has been novel tools for publishers to use to manage optimization and this will affect your ability to acquire ad inventory, so let's talk about how publisher tools evolved. I recently met with the CEO of a mid-size publisher that had a very unsophisticated tool set. He complained that the ad networks didn't like him and were deliberately sending him "low CPM campaigns". The honest truth is that this is all automated from top to bottom and understanding how the machines work and how the industry is constructed will help you understand how to extract the most value from ad networks you work with on both the buy and sell-side. This CEO's problem was not his like-ability, it was the poor technology supporting his supply-side platform.

Publishers felt overwhelmed by the growth of the ad network industry. As the networks multiplied, each network would call each publisher and ask the publisher to send them some fractional quantity of their inventory to that network. As the number of networks exploded, publishers were inundated with calls. Convention called for the publisher to be paid a share of the revenue the ad network earned based on the inventory provided by the publisher. So each network typically promised astronomically high CPMs being their norm when selling to the publisher, but in practice they usually delivered fairly low CPMs. This was no surprise as they lacked the scale of networks that had been around for a long time and inventory optimization takes time. Finding the campaigns that perform best on inventory requires testing. Further, early in a networks lifecycle, they typically had a limited base of advertisers with mixed likelihood of doing justice to a given piece of inventory. Despite this, publishers were loathe to miss out on what might be the next big thing and felt constant pressure to integrate new networks.

Publishers managed their inventory using what's called a "daisy chain". This daisy chain identified the order in which impressions should be sent to networks. The goal of the daisy chain was to send impressions in sequential order to networks most likely to generate significant revenue for the publisher. So a publisher might first monetize campaigns they sold themselves, then send impressions to their best network partner, and so on and so on.

These chains became standardized quickly coming to rely on what we call frequency segmentation. Frequency segmentation involves taking all of the traffic generated by a single user and splitting it among the networks a publisher worked with. For example, if a consumer visited a website 10 times, that website might sell the first four impressions directly itself then give the next three impressions to Network A and the final three impressions to Network B. Then if the consumer visited the website seven times,

Network B would receive zero impressions. Similarly if the consumer visited the site more frequently than additional networks would receive additional frequency slices from the publisher.

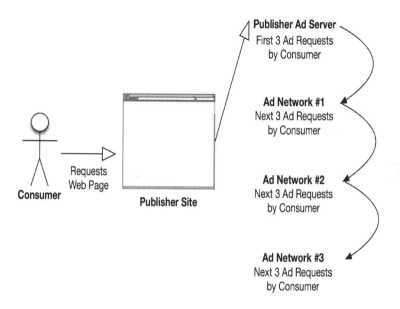

This concept of frequency management and capping was found to be important early in the advent of online advertising. If one were seeking to maximize performance for advertisers (in this case, lets assume something like clicks on the banner or conversions), showing a consumer the same ad hundreds of times was found to perform poorly. Optimal performance came only in the first few impressions. Put plainly, if they didn't click the ad in the first few impressions, they never would. So particularly in working with advertising networks that may be operating on a performance basis (such as Google), it was important to recognize the impact of frequency. This impact was also true more broadly across inventory. That is, the first ad someone saw when they came to the site, and even the first ad someone saw when they booted up their computer in the morning, would outperform subsequently viewed ads. So a network that was "higher up" in the daisy chain and saw earlier impressions would generally perform better and thus payout more for each impression to the publisher because they were receiving more performant impressions from that publisher.

Why is frequency segmentation in general and more granular, more rapid adjustment of impression allocation such an important aspect of network management? The average advertising network typically consisted of some combination of CPM campaigns and performance-based campaigns. The CPM campaigns typically had fairly high CPM's (generally north of two dollars). The performance based campaigns typically had very low CPM's – typically south of twenty five cents. These CPM campaigns usually had some sort of frequency cap. A frequency cap is a limitation on the number of times an advertisement is shown to a given user. A common frequency cap might be 3/24 – that is the ad will only be shown to a user three times in a 24-hour period. Due to the significant amount of research that has shown that exposing the user to an advertisement with very high frequency will tend to cause that advertisement to perform very poorly, if a brand advertiser chose to buy a CPM campaign from an advertising network, it generally insisted upon a frequency cap. Similarly, for the exact same performance reasons, optimization of performance-based campaigns incorporate the concept of frequency management.

In the context of simple network optimization this meant that the first time a new user was seen, a network would typically show its most valuable campaigns first followed by campaigns of declining value. This might mean for a network that the first nine impressions for a new user might represent the CPM, frequency-capped portion of the network liquidity. Following those first nine impressions, the eCPM of the network might decline rapidly as it began to show more performance-based campaigns.

How does the publisher decide which network would go first and which network would go second? Economics, of course. The publisher makes an estimate of the effective CPMs (eCPMs) for each network based on historical network performance (or simply an educated guess), and uses that to order the daisy chain. Hence an impression hops from slot to slot to slot all the way down the daisy chain. Sometimes a network might appear multiple times in the daisy chain. If a network had particularly strong performance they might receive six consecutive impressions or 10 consecutive impressions or they might appear in slot 1 and reappear in slot five (With each slot receiving 3 impressions, for example). Each publisher had their own idiosyncrasies and rules of thumb and technology capabilities for managing networks and the mechanism for managing networks varied widely from publisher to publisher.

Enter the supply side platforms. Supply-side platforms, or SSPs, promised to dramatically improve the way publishers allocated inventory to networks. By making a single massive aggregate technology investment far larger than any individual publisher could make, SSPs offered a technology stack that was uniquely valuable to publishers. At its most basic level, SSPs used technology to more efficiently allocate impressions across a set of networks and reorder that daisy chain than publishers could manually. For example, an SSP might work with an ad network to track the effective CPM of each individual frequency of user impressions sent to that network. Rather than chunking impressions in pockets of three or five to simplify the chain management process, SSP technology would allow much more granular analysis of network performance.

The goal of the SSP in maximizing publisher revenue, was to ascertain the exact amount of high value impressions a given consumer could absorb from each network. By analyzing the exact amount and value of each impression available in the network, an SSP could squeeze out of each network the maximum revenue opportunity for a given publisher.

SSPs had other advantages over the manual operations of most publishers, such as access to reporting information. A publisher might pull performance information about an ad network once a day. If they were working with many networks it might be less frequent. SSPs typically have an automated system that allows them to pull reporting information as frequently as once an hour. This allows an SSP to more effectively take advantage of the changing composition of ad network supply and demand.

Finally, SSPs typically had integrations with dozens of advertising networks. This simplified integration for publishers, decreasing the legal and integration complication publishers faced, but more importantly it increased liquidity for the publisher. The more advertising networks the publisher was dealing with, the more opportunities the publisher had to skim the cream of high CPM campaigns off the top of global advertising demand.

If you are selling advertising space on your web site, you will want to work with an SSP to sell the ad space that you cannot sell directly. They have massive technology investments in squeezing out every penny from ad networks and the breadth of their integrations gives them access to demand that might be difficult for you to tap into otherwise.

Exchanges

Supply-side platforms brought about great efficiencies for publishers, but publishers were still constrained. Publishers recognized that there were certain impressions that were uniquely valuable to specific advertising networks. For example, if a network had "cookied" a consumer at another website, that network may be willing to pay a premium for the opportunity to show an advertisement to the consumer at a later time. Unfortunately, the publisher has no way to know that the consumer had been "cookied" by the network, was valued highly by the network, whether the network had additional budget for this campaign if they had somehow known the consumer was valued, or any of a host of related questions. Much like the knowledge of what the proper mix of frequency and reach was at any given moment for an advertising network, these questions directly related to how a publisher wanted to interact with a network, but networks had no way to be transparent in this regard. Why not a standard? Because just as publishers worked with many networks, networks worked with many publishers and SSPs and this information changed moment to moment.

Right Media was the first well-known company to attempt to address this problem. They developed an advertising exchange, not dissimilar from a financial exchange in concept. The exchange allowed advertisers to place Right Media cookies, then target and bid upon those cookies as impressions with those cookies set were seen in the exchange. Right Media then went to publishers and had them place Right Media tags. This was a step improvement from SSPs in efficiency, theoretically. Now networks, rather than having a theoretically optimal place in the daisy chain assigned by algorithms, could configure a bid for every impression sent to the network and associate value with that bid. For example, if a network was placing a cookie on consumers that visited an e-commerce site, they could replace that cookie with a Right Media cookie (or more accurately, supplement) then bid on impressions where that cookie was set in the Right Media exchange.

This was a sea change for the online advertising business. Previously, scale played a huge role in the development of advertising networks. As we discussed earlier, it was far more meaningful to a publisher if a network had the ability to monetize large volumes of impressions somewhat efficiently than monetize a small amount of impressions very efficiently. For a network to be high in the daisy chain of a publisher or SSP, they needed to be able to take almost any impression and turn it into reliable revenue. With the advent of exchanges, suddenly a business that had previously been shut out of publisher inventory due to limited scale had opportunities.

Consider this: Previously, I had told you how easy it was to call some advertisers and start your own advertising network. I mentioned that the key to success at that point was that you simply had to perform. This is true, but performance was difficult because the constraint at that moment was access to inventory. If you called a publisher and asked for inventory, they might slice you off a frequency range and send it to you, but then you had to make that inventory work. Typically, you would start at the back of the daisy chain and had to deliver high CPMs to move up in the chain. If you were starting your business, with just a few advertisers, this was difficult. Consider this model:

Advertiser CTR by Publisher

	Pub 1	Pub 2	Pub 3	Pub 4
Advertiser 1	1.00%	0.54%	0.34%	0.24%
Advertiser 2	0.68%	0.73%	0.23%	0.74%
Advertiser 3	0.39%	0.61%	1.34%	1.01%
Advertiser 4	0.85%	0.35%	0.78%	0.12%

This shows how different advertisers might perform, absent other information on a variety of publishers. That is, this is a silly table filled with random numbers because the interactions are generally uncorrelated. If a new network was built around some cookie based targeting, they were at the mercy of the publisher to hope and pray that impressions sent to them had the appropriate cookies set (there was basically no way for a publisher to know since they cannot look at another domain's cookies). If the targeting was inventory-based, there was no way to know, in advance, how that inventory would perform.

In fact, even if the targeting were cookie-based, different inventory still performs differently. This could reflect the engagement of the user (e.g. If the consumer was playing a game vs. reading news vs. checking a social network) or it could reflect the advertisements position on the page (e.g. "Above the fold" – an advertisement that is in the consumers view when the page loads vs. "Below the fold" – an advertisement that the consumer must scroll the page to bring into view. (A concept stolen from the newspaper industry.)). A million other variables could be at play in any given situation, but suffice it to say that different inventory performs differently for different creatives. Some of these variances remain true regardless of creatives, for example many casual games are designed to place an advertisement near where the user clicks in the game, this engenders high click rates across every kind of ad as consumers accidentally click the ad while playing the game. This is also typically true for a site's home page where the advertisement viewed is usually in a premium position and early in a users session, resulting in higher engagement and performance. Conversely, some variation in performance is directly related to the relationship between the banner and the site. For example, advertisements for financial services might perform much better on a page about financial planning than an advertisement to join a social network. The relevance creates performance.

Regardless, as our hypothetical model indicates, performance will vary across inventory sources for a given advertiser. If a newborn network has very few advertisers participating in the network, it will typically be difficult to ensure that a publishers inventory is used to its best ability. To the extent that the inventory is poorly used, the advertiser is displeased and the CPMs are typically lower (to the extent the campaign is performance-based). This incents the publisher to discontinue the use of said network, testing the next network to come along. Also, it causes the advertiser to perform poorly, decreasing the long-term success of the network. As a network grew, it could reach a critical mass where it saw enough cookies to enable it to sell cookie-based targeting, but when a network had few advertisers, its aggregate monetization of the average, unremarkable impressions prevented it from offering cookie-based targeting as publishers would not pass it sufficient inventory (and sufficiently early impressions in the user experience) to allow it to create value.

Hence, SSPs and static daisy chains had an unintentionally chilling effect on the growth of targeting and the expansion of advertising tools. The inability of small networks to acquire the inventory they needed for targeting, particularly as cookie-based targeting opened new avenues of targeting opportunity, was an obstacle to the evolution of Internet advertising.

The exchange-based approach was a novel solution to this problem. Each publisher could contribute impressions to the exchange. As the exchange received an impression, it would look at a collection of rules, pre-defined by each advertiser. The rules defined the bid placed by an advertiser for a given impression opportunity. Each impression was then auctioned to the highest bidder, the bid defined by the rules from each advertiser.

Example bid rules might include something like:
- US-only impression
- Daily budget cap of $100
- Has a Right Media cookie value of X (some custom identifier created by the advertiser)
- No casual gaming or pornographic inventory

Right Media grew slowly out of the gate: While this auction model conceptually offered an opportunity to create marginally higher CPMs for a given impression, this was only true if there were enough advertisers bidding on the inventory to create this value. Many small ad networks and their like joined Right Media quickly, but larger ad networks, which had the bulk of advertisers at that time, moved very slowly. Contributing to the exchanges success would create an intermediary between them and the SSPs and publishers and force them to compete on a dimension other than massive reach (for advertisers) and broad monetization capabilities (for publishers), the prior focus of most of these businesses.

Similarly, publishers were slow to adopt Right Media's novel platform. With few advertisers initially, Right Media faced the same problem that a small ad network would face: When a publisher tried them, the CPMs were low. Very large ad networks, with their own internal auction and a critical mass of advertisers were able to deliver higher CPMs.

Over time, Right Media and DoubleClick (who had started a competing exchange) grew (with Right Media being acquired for $800 million by Yahoo! and DoubleClick being acquired by Google for $3 billion), but there was an even more dramatic transition underway: The transition to real-time bidding.

While exchanges were a huge asset to many advertisers, the rules that an advertiser needed to load into each exchange could be burdensome and cause challenges for the advertiser. For example, they assumed that the advertiser was only buying inventory through the exchange. If the advertiser wanted to place a buy in more than one exchange or was working across many publishers in addition to the exchange (as was common for ad networks working in exchanges), the concept that the exchange had a "budget" presented challenges. The "buy" was completely disconnected from the other processes of the ad network. For example, if an advertiser had given the network an order for 1,000,000 impressions with a special targeting parameter, the network would be generally indifferent to where those 1,000,000 impressions were delivered. Unfortunately, it would need to designate a budget that was difficult to manage and somewhat inflexible for the exchange. The network did not want to carve out a dedicated exchange budget. It wanted to manage the exchange similar to how it managed other publishers, evaluating each impression in real time and selecting the most appropriate advertiser for it. Similarly if the insertion order (IO, the parlance for an order in the industry) designated a frequency cap, the frequency cap was impossible to manage across multiple exchanges. (e.g. If you were contractually restricted to showing a consumer three ads per 24 hour period, but were running the ad in 2 exchanges, the only way you could control delivery was doing a 1/24 frequency cap in one and a 2/24 cap in another, unnaturally de-optimizing delivery.)

Real-time Bidding (or RTB), offered a solution to this that was both elegant and effective. In real-time bidding, when an ad impression arrived at the exchange, it was "shared" with the bidders, each of which could look at the impression (allowing them to see their cookies) and place a bid. The highest bidder subsequently won the auction and received the impression. This allowed bidders to change how much they bid for impressions in real-time, control their bidding algorithms, and have more insight into bid activity.

Demand Side Platforms

Invite Media was founded by Nate Turner and Zach Weinberg, two recent college graduates from the University of Pennsylvania. While Invite had gone through a number of pivots (the original notion is hinted at by their name), the business they quickly arrived at was providing a bidding platform for ad agencies to access inventory on exchanges. The industry came to call this a Demand Side Platform (DSP).

Previously, ad agencies had two ways to have their ads shown on a web site:

1) Execute a buy with a specific site. For example, buying 100,000 impressions on ESPN.

2) Execute a buy with a specific ad network. For example, buying 100,000 impressions through ValueClick, which

would be spread across a collection of sites the network acquired inventory from.

If the goal was to reach large numbers of users and have high performance, working with networks was an important part of the buy.

1) It was much less expensive than a direct buy because networks paid significantly below rate card to acquire inventory.

2) Because they reached across sites, they were able to get access to large numbers of people. Going direct to a site to get reach like this required buying the most premium inventory; the Yahoo! home page was a good example of an expensive way to get very high performance reach.

3) Networks were able to quickly pivot into strong performance. If one site had low click-through rates and one site had high click-through rates, the network could take advantage of real-time data to make a real-time decision and shift the inventory distribution for a campaign towards a high performer. Ad agencies would have to go through a time consuming process of getting reports on campaign performance, cancel buys with poor performers, and place new buys to shift budgets.

But networks were not a joy to work with because there was little to no transparency or control over the buy once an agency gave the money to the network. Generally, networks provided no insight into where a buy would run, how many impressions would run on each site, or how any of those sites performed for the buy. This was necessary to preserve the networks marketplace: If an agency could call the network and say, "I want 100,000 impressions on ESPN.com", then the network would be directly competing with the site for ad sales.

If ESPN found out that a network they provided inventory to was competing with them for a sale and directly representing their inventory, the typical strategy for ESPN, or any publisher, was to cut off inventory supply to the network. As previously discussed, the incremental revenue from any given network was generally not significant compared to one sizable direct sales opportunity and a publisher typically felt (correctly, I suspect) that if they had found out about this kind of direct competition in this one instance, there were probably dozens more that the publisher was unaware of.

There were exceptions to this kind of channel conflict: Rep networks, or networks that directly represented and sold bundles of inventory on behalf of publishers, were not uncommon, but they typically worked with smaller publishers that did not have direct sales force scale. The publishers that had inventory that agencies were most interested in directly buying were also the largest – Yahoo!, AOL, MySpace (remember them?), and other well-known brands. These brands had huge volumes of inventory, more than they could ever sell themselves, but they also had large direct sales forces. They had no need to work with rep networks or risk their competition. Instead, they preferred to sell their inventory to performance networks that were required to sell inventory on a "blind" basis: We can't tell you where you ran, or how much you ran on those sites, we can only report blind, aggregate data to protect our publishers.

We have talked about the tradeoffs for publishers already, but this put agencies in an awkward position: They had to trust the network when the network said, "We can't tell you where your ad will run because it will run on such incredibly reputable sites that the sites will not let us tell you what they are for fear that you will never work with them again when you realize how much of their inventory we have and how cheaply we are able to procure it." And inevitably, they would find instances where their trust was misplaced. Some networks, due to the challenge of accessing truly top-tier inventory would tell that story, then run the campaign on much lower quality inventory. Yes, including porn – an agencies worst nightmare.

Technology solutions sprang up to address this: Third party verification services that attempted to root out where ads ran. But the Demand Side Platform, the ability for agencies to have their own technology stack to control RTB buying, was a solution that truly addressed the market need in a novel way and agencies quickly embraced it.

Further and maybe more importantly, agencies were interested in margins. Most ad networks had approximately 40% margins – they paid the publisher 60% of the revenue they generated. That told agencies that nearly half of every dollar they spent on ad networks was earned by the network providing a marketplace. If a combination of exchange and DSP technology allowed the agency to disintermediate the network, then the network might be able to keep some of that marginal revenue for themselves. If an agency was charging a 15% fee for media planning, if they were able to justify keeping 40% of the remaining 85% (by contributing network services), that could significantly change the marginal value of media planning to an agency.

With a Demand Side Platform, an agency could work with the DSP to identify what inventory they wanted to buy, how much they wanted to pay for that inventory, and how they wanted the buy managed. They could get as much or as little reporting as they wanted, but they felt like they were in control. DSPs built user interfaces (UIs) called "trading desks" that allowed the agency to use a self-service system to manage the buy themselves. The DSP had no incentive to keep relationships in the exchange blind. If the exchange gave them access to information, they would use it.

The DSPs were a hit with agencies and most agencies embarked on building out their own internal trading desk operations. Some built their own technology, some white-labeled DSP technology from start-ups. All of them started grooming specialist teams that evaluated DSP technology, understood how to use DSPs and managed DSP relationships.

Today, many advertisers are disintermediating agencies and building their own internal trading desks to claw back the margin for themselves. Studies indicate that more than 11% of programmatic spend in 2013 was advertisers trading their own business[23].

Now, for our purposes, working with networks is probably fine. Transparency is not as important as strong performance. All of these exchanges sell their inventory on a CPM basis so using an intermediary like a network that is willing to take a buy from us on a CPC or CPA basis and assume the performance risk is better than controlling delivery site by site. If a network can generate 40% margins while meeting our metrics, good for them. The need to manage our own exchange buying is mitigated by the desire to have other parties assume the performance risk for our advertising.

Creatives

Until now, virtually this entire tome has been devoted to reaching the right audience. How it works, how to do it, and how to think about that problem. Unfortunately, that is less than half the battle. Creative quality and messaging account for a huge portion of performance associated with any given campaign. Regardless of how well a campaign is targeted, its overall success will depend heavily on the strength of the creative.

Some ads may appeal more to particular demographics and work better in particular contexts or among people at different stages in the purchase process. If these creative variations are understood in advance, the campaign can be planned accordingly.

Many technology platforms have been built to create dynamic or rich media ads to create more effective ads. While this is important, equally important is finding a way to reach out and really have a meaningful impact on the consumer.

When I first joined Advertising.com, one of the calculations that led me to join was that it seemed like the market was poised for explosive growth, far above and beyond expectations. Here was my off-the-cuff theory:

- Online was 5% of US media spend
- Online was 17% of US media consumption
- Until those two numbers are the same, people are getting better value advertising online than anywhere else (arbitrage), so those two numbers will gradually come into alignment.

That made me think that the market would grow 20%+ YoY for several years, because I didn't think that 17% would get any smaller.

Lo and behold, I was right about that, at least. Today the numbers are headed in the right direction:

- 12% of US media spend is online
- 30% of US media consumption is online

So, far from coming together, these two numbers, while increasing rapidly, are actually diverging.

My new theory as to why this is: Advertising online is simply not as good as it should be. Many professional creative advertisers find that for their purposes, online advertising simply doesn't work as well as advertising on TV. So TV is getting a disproportionate amount of advertising dollars relative to its media consumption. And that is not too surprising. 728x90s feel limited. They don't tell a story. They are like tiny magazine ads.

TV ads have a story arc. They have punch lines. They are visually stimulating.

Targeting and measurability and all the stuff that most people in online advertising do is great. They create a situation where advertising theoretically could work better by being more personalized. Flight prices to Vegas from your city are not what we are talking about, though. Without a fundamental change in the kinds of creatives that big brands can put out there, online ads simply won't work as well, at least in a subjective sense for brand advertisers.

Solving this problem is hard.

First, we must overcome prohibitive expense. People already spend way more outside of buying media when prepping an online campaign then they ever did for TV. You build some web site with some viral thing on it, and all that stuff. That is great. If a consumer wants to engage with your brand, you want that brand experience to be awesome. But the first step in engagement is seeing an awesome ad. If you asked the top X agencies today if they would prefer a consumers first interaction with a brand be via a 160×600 or a 30 second spot, I think you would struggle to get anyone to say the web banner. Making these great ads is expensive though and someone has to do it.

Second, there must be a visionary industry breakthrough. Even if we knew how to do it all affordably, I don't know that we would crack the nut anyway. What do awesome ads look like? Punch the monkey captured the imagination. I just named a 728×90 ad that people actually recognize (although I don't know what they were selling). Dancing Lower My Bills ads? These caught the eye but in a way that left me angry and bitter. I don't think Teracent or Tumri (companies that specialize in algorithmic creative optimization) are solving this problem. Making the ad green or blue or blue-green may increase the odds that I click, but it doesn't vault the ad into the pantheon of great advertising moments. At least not mine.

Everything that I see in the market is evolutionary and incremental, but this is not the time for incremental. We are in the first inning. You are not standing on the shoulders of giants, you are standing on a speck of dust. There is so much room for change that we need people to swing for the fences.

Let this be a call to entrepreneurs. If you figure out how to make great ads online, you get a billion dollars.

Are We Trading Stocks Now?

Particularly with the emergence of exchanges, many have equated the development of online advertising with the stock market. They imagine a world where impressions are bought and sold much like stocks with programmatic systems.

Unfortunately for our industry, this corollary does not hold well. While the display advertising market is a tiny fraction of the size of the stock market, the trading of impressions is much more complex. Generally, a share of stock is quite fungible. If you have a share of AT&T, it is exactly the same as all of the other shares of

AT&T. A share of stock has a price. An ad impression is fairly unique: An advertisement shown at 1:00 AM has different performance characteristics than an advertisement shown at 1:00 PM, even on the same site. Different consumers have different frequencies with which they have viewed ads, different histories with respect to their likelihood of clicking an ad, and different browsers, operating systems, and historical data profiles. When you have an ad impression from Neopets.com, bidding on it without regard to many other data points makes valuing that impression difficult.

That suits us fine: Not just anyone can jump in here and do the things that we are doing with advertising. This helps us create competitive barriers for our products. Part of our market value will be our effectiveness at valuing marketing opportunities.

Adult Influence on Internet Advertising

No discussion of the digital world would be complete without at least a passing reference to the role of pornography. Many people think of pornography as a technology vanguard: They led the way in the adoption of technology such as VHS players and DVDs. Similarly, they have led in many aspects of Internet technology development: Video, group chat, streaming video and advertising. Adult entertainment is also currently leading the way into a critical new revenue stream for content sites: paywalls and micropayments

Adult entertainment is a huge industry. Here are a few data points for reference:

- 12% of web sites on the Internet are pornographic in nature.
- The porn industry makes $3,000 per second online.
- There are 40 million monthly consumers of porn in the U.S.
- 25% of all search-engine queries are porn related.[24]

Advertising in pornography today is remarkably sophisticated, but it is easy to understand why: There is a large financial opportunity and it is being pursued by people that are only interested in money. They aren't interested in developing their brand, they are interested in money.

Adult sites tend to be meticulously organized, with sections and subsections that allow for extremely targeted advertising using the age or race of the actors. The ads tend to be extremely intrusive: Pop-up ads and pre-roll videos with rich media are the dominant form of creative. Strong calls to action and interactive or faux-interactive advertisements. Related videos and other kinds of advertorial content are thoughtfully placed to maximize engagement.

Finally, the adult industry invented the affiliate advertising business and today has some of the most complex affiliate advertising schemes as traffic is driven from micro-site to micro-site.

I don't think this stuff has much relevance to what we are doing, but if I didn't mention it, then you might say I didn't mention it. You can probably see how a lot of what these sites do is based on the principles we have talked about.

Real-time Bidding

The RTB Revolution

Now you understand the history of how the economics of digital advertising evolved. Let's take a quick moment to bring it up to the present day and talk about ways we can use cash in real time attention auctions to help us sell products.

Real-time bidding (RTB) is programmatic buying of advertising inventory in which these digital advertising opportunities are auctioned off in real-time. The auctions take place in milliseconds as advertisers bid on the right to show you an ad immediately after you open an app or click to a new web page and reminds many of the sophistication of high-frequency trading on Wall Street. RTB enables buyers and sellers to dynamically adjust their bids and asks as market conditions change and also based on real-time feedback on the effectiveness of an ad campaign.

RTB has enabled a single platform to connect to multiple disparate inventory sources and make real-time buying decisions on each impression-by-impression. Buying decisions are thus powerfully transferred from the inventory vendor directly to the actual media buyer.

Real-time bidding is probably the most powerful trend changing advertising (not just digital advertising), hence no discussion of advertising would be complete without spending some more time talking about it. RTB has only been available since late 2009, but it is rapidly attracting more spending and gaining market share because it is much more efficient than traditional forms of programmatic trading.

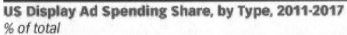

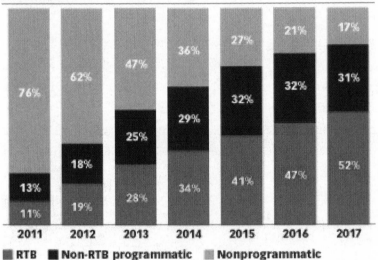

US Display Ad Spending Share, by Type, 2011-2017
% of total

	2011	2012	2013	2014	2015	2016	2017
Nonprogrammatic	76%	62%	47%	36%	27%	21%	17%
Non-RTB programmatic	13%	18%	25%	29%	32%	32%	31%
RTB	11%	19%	28%	34%	41%	47%	52%

■ RTB ■ Non-RTB programmatic ■ Nonprogrammatic

Note: read as 28% of display-related spending was through RTB in 2013; numbers may not add up to 100% due to rounding
Source: MAGNA GLOBAL as cited in press release, Oct 14, 2013
164874   www.eMarketer.com[25]

IDC recently announced a study that looked at RTB market growth and it was dramatic. They noted that:

> RTB spend will continue its rapid growth as a percentage of digital advertising spending, rising from a respectable 14% in 2013 to a massive 41% over the next four years in the United States, and from 8% to 28% worldwide.
>
> While the United States will remain the most mature and advanced market for programmatic spending, growing at an anticipated average rate of 48% a year from $2 billion in 2012 to a predicted $14.4 billion in 2017, other markets are poised for rapid growth as well.

IDC's research predicts that the Western European market will grow
from $381 million in 2012, to $3.3 billion in 2017, with RTB's display advertising spend share rising from 5% to 23%, while Japan's programmatic spending will grow from $218 million to $1.1 billion with advertising spend share
rising from 5% to 28%.[26]

In the past, if this media buyer wanted to buy media, they
would work with a provider like Right Media, ValueClick, Google
or one of the tens of thousands of publishers and ad networks out
there. Ad buys were achieved by either inputting rules-based buying instructions on various fragmented interfaces, working with
an account rep, or using an API to communicate with an ad server. Once these buying instructions were defined, a provider would
serve an ad, and make a buy, when an impression occurred on that
particular network or site fit within the defined criteria. Buyers
could then log in to the exchange to run reports, optimize campaigns or make minor tweaks and changes.

Media buyers (and their clients) who needed mass impression
inventory would have to perform this task over dozens, if not
hundreds, of sources to achieve scale, since in this highly fragmented space no provider had a dominant share of the inventory.
A big agency could work with as many as a thousand digital media
vendors when you count the publishers, exchanges, ad networks,
and intermediaries. Suddenly, buyers were logging into numerous
interfaces, pulling and collating disparate reports and are left
trusting dozens of black boxes to run their ads in the right places.
Very simply, the fragmentation in the display space made digital
media buying a nightmare. Moreover, the vendor was in control
of where the ads actually ran, which inhibited transparency and
targeting for the buyer.

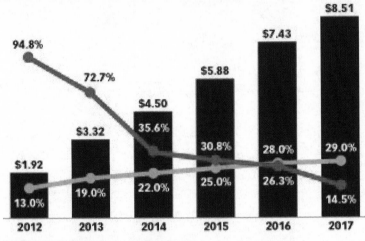

US Real-Time Bidding (RTB) Digital Display Ad Spending, 2012-2017
billions, % change and % of total digital display ad spending

- ■ RTB digital display ad spending
- ■ % change ■ % of total digital display ad spending

Note: includes all display formats served to all devices
Source: eMarketer, June 2013

157509   www.eMarketer.com[27]

Exchanges change much of this. Instead of each individual media buyer having to learn and rely on an incongruous collection of their vendors' ad software, they can instead use a single platform to manage buying all in one place. This single platform aggregates multiple inventory sources, making it possible to target very narrowly defined audience segments at scale using a single standard without fear of overlap. RTB has taken it a step further. Buyers can now use data they have collected and developed about their customers' target users and communicate with those users directly as individuals. The modes of buying shift from targeting inventory sources to targeting individual users, and in turn, audiences.

As you scale your business to work with networks, increasingly these networks don't own any of their own inventory or have a significant number of direct relationships. They buy their inventory through the exchanges to get greater reach. You can ask them which exchanges they work with, how many impressions they see each day, and what the meaningful reach of their network via exchanges looks like. Even relatively small industry players will look at more than one billion impressions per day.

Similarly, as you scale, you may have the opportunity to work directly with exchanges, although exchanges are less likely to be interested in assuming performance risk. The result is that using network optimization will be the most efficient way, particularly in the early-going, to achieve your financial targets.

Private Marketplaces

Exchanges present many sources of consternation for publishers. Concerns that they could cannibalize the direct sales of publishers is chief among those. Secondarily, they worry that the exchange cheapens and commoditizes their inventory.

To alleviate publishers' concerns, SSP/exchanges began to offer them "private marketplaces", a special exchange run just for the publisher which runs on the RTB platforms, but which offers the publisher more control. The private marketplace is then restricted to just one or few publishers and a select set of buyers permitted by the publisher or group of publishers. They also offer greater control over pricing and over which advertisers and advertisements are featured on a publisher's site. Thus private marketplaces address publishers' two major concerns around RTB: protecting their current price levels and making sure no inappropriate ads run on their services.

For example, the New York Times created a private marketplace which became the only way to RTB bid on their inventory. The New York Times was able to keep tight controls over bids placed on their inventory and who was allowed to place those bids to ensure that they had high quality advertisers. They also used this to try to convince those advertisers to bid higher prices than they may have bid in the broader exchange to access this "special" inventory source.

Working with very large networks will probably be the most effective way for a start-up to get access to these private markets. Those markets are great sources of high performing inventory because they represent high quality publishers.

Advertiser Technology Under Scrutiny

I won't walk through an example of exactly how RTB works at the protocol level, but I will give you a high level understanding of how it typically works.

1. The ad impression comes into the exchange.
2. The exchange selects several bidders who are likely to bid on the inventory and forwards them information about the bid request
3. Bidders each return a bid, the ad that they will show if they win the bid, and a URL for the exchange to call to notify them that they won the bid.
4. The exchange selects the highest bidder, shows their ad, and calls the winning URL.

This essentially follows the outline of the OpenRTB standard[28], the most widely adopted approach to RTB. In other approaches, the ad does not necessarily need to be sent in the response, the exchange simply redirects the impression to the winner.

RTB has changed the balance of technological sophistication required by buyers and sellers of ad inventory. It used to be that ad buyers only had to operate on impressions they bought. Now they need to look at bid requests and decide what they are worth prior to buying. And that decision needs to be made in less than 100 milliseconds. Ad buying technology is changing quickly.

The ad sellers world has not changed nearly as much. Most ad sellers had a yield optimizer before that algorithmically guessed about how the daisy chain should be arranged. Now they simply RTB the impression. The technology used by the yield optimizer has actually gotten much simpler – there is no longer any optimization. You simply take the impression and RTB it. Instead of guessing who will pay the most and sending the impression to them, you share the impression the impression with everyone and see who will pay the most. There is less need for calculation, learning or consideration of past performance.

This means that for startups that are looking for online advertising capabilities, it is important to find partners that can provide this kind of optimization support. Otherwise, they risk ending up with the impressions that other people didn't want to buy. These could be the poor performers. Let's talk next about how that decision happens.

Header Bidding

Header bidding represents the evolution of RTB technology and publisher strategies. We have talked about how replacing waterfall network allocations with auctioning improves publisher yield. But there is still a waterfall occurring! First, the impressions go to the publisher ad server to determine if they have direct sold campaigns that need to be filled. Then the impressions go to the SSP or exchange to be auctioned if they are not needed for direct served campaigns.

Philosophically, this sounds like motherhood and apple pie: If I told an advertiser I would deliver a campaign for them and we have a relationship and they are typically paying premium CPMs, then of course I want to make sure I am delivering that campaign before I consider auctioning it off "remnant-style".

But there are problems with this. Some of those impressions are, without a doubt, extremely valuable on the spot market. For example, this consumer was just shopping for a new car on Cars.com. While in general, the auction bids might tend to be below the CPM generally offered via direct deals, a consumer like this might be more valuable in the spot market than they are to the advertisers we have partnered with directly.

Further, in the context of filling our direct campaigns as a publisher, these impressions may be quite fungible. If we knew that the spot market placed a premium value on this impression, we would sell this impression on the spot market and keep some other impression that we had planned to auction.

So if we were able to identify inordinately valuable impressions before deciding whether it should have ads generated by the publisher ad server or the open market, we could increase yield.

So how does one accomplish such amazing things? Header bidding. In header bidding, when the page loads, before the ad is decisioned, javascript is fired off that gives the exchange a chance to inform the ad server what the impression would be worth in the exchange. Similarly, the ad server interrogates the publisher ad server and determines what the impression would be worth to publisher advertisers. Then it determines who should receive the impression and resolves it.

An obvious concern would be that direct campaigns may not be filled, but this can be easily alleviated by modulating the bid by the publisher ad server or some other flag if a campaign is at risk, but the opportunity to capture incremental revenue fairly easily is difficult to pass up. Also, publishers have already come to terms with this in many respects because they use header bidding already in another way: DFP, Google's publisher ad server, has a "dynamic allocation" setting that allows impressions to receive bids from the Google ad exchange. Header bidding creates an open standard that allows publishers to experiment with other ad exchanges.

The other challenge of header bidding is the added page load time. Given the impact on SEO, a publisher should be very careful about how they execute header bidding and the impact it has on page bloat.

Finally, header bidding creates a complication for exchanges. Today many exchanges, including Google, use second price auctions. A second price auction allows all parties to bid for inventory, then the highest bidder wins, but pays the price of the second bidder. Theoretically, this encourages parties to not be conservative in their bidding because they know that even if they bid high, if they win they will pay a lower price. The nominal goal is to ensure that all parties are paying at or near their LCV rather than experimenting with different bid prices to achieve greater cost savings. While historically this has been very successful, header bidding complicates this. With header bidding, a situation could arise where the highest bid in an exchange could be enough to win the impression relative to the publisher ad server, but the second highest price might not be! This challenges advertisers and exchanges to consider their business models: On the one hand, if the market moved to a more traditional auction, gaming the auction would be a technology burden for advertisers. Conversely, if advertisers were indeed willing to pay the first price and losing inventory opportunities because their bid is not represented, that would represent a squandered opportunity for all concerned.

Despite this, header bidding appears to be the wave of the future in evolving the advertising technology stack for publishers. Google reports that their early tests indicate that publisher revenue increases by approximately 10%.[29] That is a significant opportunity that publishers will seize.

Bring on the Math

How Ad Display Works

Before I turn this knowledge of industry players into a definitive buying strategy, I want to talk about what we are buying and how we show ads. A lot of people will offer you and I the opportunity to buy some ads with them in a way that sounds perfectly reasonable but is designed for you to lose your shirt. These ads might be viewed by a robot programmatically surfing the Internet, be displayed on a location on the page that is actually impossible to view with a browser, or even, with the best intentioned publisher, simply not properly display on the publisher page.

There are a couple of ways to avoid this. One, as I constantly emphasize, is to buy on a performance basis. Generally, although there are exceptions, these ads do not perform, no matter how many you show. Of course, some generate clicks that are not real. So we need to be on guard for that. These are all things that can hit you right in the pocketbook, so if we know how ad display actually works, you can recognize some of these pitfalls.

You know how HTML works. Let's turn that into ad knowledge. Here is an example of an ad tag that a publisher could put in their HTML page:

```
<script type="text/javascript"
src="http://c.vrvm.com/pass/vrv/adtag/vervetag.j
s?partner=example"></script>
```

This is a basic ad tag. It is something that a publisher can drop into a page wherever they want an ad to appear. They might pop it into an iframe, they might not. That is really the publisher perogative.

In this case, the ad tag is a javascript script. So when you put this on a page, when it gets to this ad tag, it runs the script located at this source: "http://c.vrvm.com/pass/vrv/adtag/vervetag.js". It includes a parameter that identifies the partner (in this case "example") so an ad appropriate to that partner could be returned. Frequently other parameters such as the size of the ad or the genre of content being consumed are passed, but this is a good start. This javascript, when executed, likely returns some HTML. It might look like this:

```
HTTP/1.1 200 OK
Date: Fri, 31 Dec 2012 23:59:59 GMT
Content-Type: text/html

<A HREF="http://www.nissan.com/">
<IMG
SRC="http://www.nissan.com/picture_of_car.gif">
</A>
```

So this ad tag is a script that retrieves HTML from the c.vrvm.com server and then displays it wherever the tag was placed.

What is exciting about the ad tags is that they are non-specific! This tag could return any ad. So the publisher has a generic snippet of HTML that they use to let the ad server know to return an ad, then the ad server is free to return an appropriate ad of any sort. For example, if, on the request, the ad server realized that this consumer had already seen the Nissan ad (by cookie inspection), it could dynamically return a different ad. This is an abstraction that is useful in many aspects of the Internet, but particularly so in the world of online advertising.

As long as we are nerding out, we can complicate the example to think through all the things a smart online advertiser thinks about. Let's start small. A smarter response from the ad server might include something like this:

```
<A
HREF="http://click.vrvm.com/?www.nissan.com/">
<IMG
SRC="http://www.nissan.com/picture_of_car.gif">
</A>
```

When a consumer clicks on the link, instead of going to nissan.com, it goes to click.vrvm.com. This is the "click server" for the ad server. The click server's job is simple: It allows the ad server to track that a click has taken place. The click.vrvm.com server gets a request from the consumer, logs that request in its log files and then the server responds with a 301 redirect to www.nissan.com.

Now that we have introduced one redirect, we can come to grips with the fact that redirects could be strung together in a chain. The publisher might use a third party remnant network optimizer (an SSP, or "Supply Side Platform") that provides them with some ad tags. Those ad tags call the SSP which determines that Ad Network X is most likely to have a high paying ad at that moment. So when the SSP is called by the publisher page, the SSP responds with a 301 redirect to Ad Network X. Ad Network X sees the ad and determines that an advertisement for Coca-Cola is the best ad to serve. However, the ad agency for Coca-Cola has placed a buy with 5 ad networks for their latest Coca-Cola campaign, so they are using their own ad server to serve up the campaign so they can track how many total ads have been shown at any point in time across all of the networks. So Ad Network X, rather than having the actual Coke ad, simply has another URL to redirect the campaign to, provided by the ad agency. So they use a 301 redirect to send the request to the ad agency ad server, which returns the Coca-Cola ad.

It's a good thing you are an online advertising geek or this would sound like total nonsense! But what we just heard was a super important concept, so let's look at a picture that walks us through it:

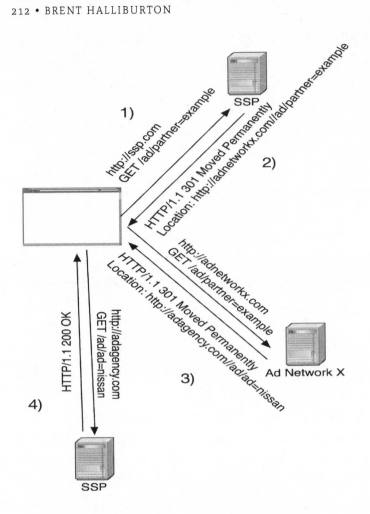

That is a lot of arrows, but the logic is straightforward:

1. The Publisher sends the request to the SSP
2. The SSP picks the right ad network to fill the ad and responds to the client with a redirect
3. The ad network picks the right advertiser to pick the ad and responds to the client with a redirect
4. The advertiser receives the request for an ad and responds with that ad

And typically all of this happens in less than a few hundred milliseconds.

Let me wrap this up with one last bit of complexity: How does anyone know that an advertisement was actually displayed? There is no perfect way to really know. If you consider it for a moment, what you would like to do is take a screenshot of the consumers screen, however that is technically very difficult. Alternately, you could have the advertiser go to the publishers site and try to see the ad, but the probability that the daisy chain of activity is the same from request to request is very small. Another approach, called the "viewable impression" is to write javascript that tries to detect if the ad is in the browser window or is "below the fold" when displayed. There is significant investment in this area, however due to differences in browsers and underlying technology, it is non-trivial work and not widespread today.

Instead, what is conventional in the industry is to "impression count". In impression counting, we assume that an image was displayed if an image file is requested by a client. For example, in our original example we have a tag for an image file called: http://www.nissan.com/picture_of_car.gif. If we look in our log files for requests that are made for that file, that means that the ad server returned that ad and then the client asked for the appropriate image. If a consumer went to a page and then left that page before the ad was requested, the request for the image is never seen by the server and recorded in the log files. By parsing the log files for actual ad requests for the image, it is possible to determine the difference between times that the ad response was served and times that the image file in the response was actually displayed.

The logging and redirection is extended in impression counting as third parties interconnect. Each of these parties: Publisher, SSP, Ad Network, and Ad Agency Ad Server all have a vested interest in tracking the ad displays. But the actual image file is only hosted by the last party. (In fact, many times the Ad Agency ad server is not hosting the image! It might be stored on an Amazon Web Services CDN or some other distributed framework to make downloading that file faster.) So what they do is add a pixel.

Pixels are a simple tool that fills an important need in the ad serving universe in this respect. A pixel is a 1x1 image; that is, a 1 pixel high, 1 pixel wide graphical image so small that it cannot generally be seen. When ad servers are using a pixel to count impressions, rather than returning a simple redirect, they return a tag that provides the redirection manually, plus a pixel. So if the SSP wants to redirect to an ad network, and then track whether an image was requested, it might respond to an ad request with a response like this:

```
HTTP/1.1 200 OK
Date: Fri, 31 Dec 2012 23:59:59 GMT
Content-Type: text/html

<script type="text/javascript"
src="http://c.vrvm.com/pass/vrv/adtag/vervetag.j
s?ptnr=example"></script>
<IMG SRC="http://ssp.com/pixel?adid=12345">
```

Now, the script that called the SSP server responded with HTML that caused another script to be requested from the vrvm ad network and appended to that response their pixel.

Then the vrvm ad network might respond with something like this:

```
HTTP/1.1 200 OK
Date: Fri, 31 Dec 2012 23:59:59 GMT
Content-Type: text/html

<A HREF="http://www.nissan.com/">
<IMG
SRC="http://www.nissan.com/picture_of_car.gif">
</A>
<IMG SRC="http://vrvm.com/pixel?adid=abcdef">
```

So now they have shown Nissan's ad and appended their pixel. So if someone looked at the source code in the browser, the rendered HTML they would see from the execution of the initial SSP tag may look like:

```
<A HREF="http://www.nissan.com/">
<IMG
SRC="http://www.nissan.com/picture_of_car.gif">
</A>
<IMG SRC="http://vrvm.com/pixel?adid=abcdef">
<IMG SRC="http://ssp.com/pixel?adid=12345">
```

Both the SSP and vrvm have images attached to the final response and they can search through their request logs to see how many consumers requested the ad ID they assigned to that request and they will know whether that response resulted in the ad actually being displayed. This concept of using a random identifier such as an ad ID allows a one to one connection to be made between a specific ad request and an ad being displayed and could be unique to a publisher/network relationship, an ad campaign, or even an ad request.

Now the SSP, the Ad Network, and the advertiser all can confirm that the publisher actually displayed the ad to the consumer. Similarly, we discussed click tracking earlier. Many SSPs and networks have standards that allow a "click-tracker" to be inserted into their ad tags, so that a click can be "passed" by 301 redirection from SSP to network to advertiser so all parties can recognize that a click took place and track the performance of inventory.

Typically, in the world of ad serving, people talk about "discrepancy" with some frequency. Discrepancy is the difference in counts between, in this example, the SSP and and ad server, or any two parties. Discrepancies occur for many reasons, but the most common is simply that in between the two requests, the consumer browsed to another page or stopped the page load for some other reason. Conventional wisdom is that a discrepancy of less than 10% is probably fine.

You just completed your ad serving merit badge!

How Ad Decisioning Works

The next big step towards creating an advertising powerhouse is to bring on the math. To have a complete understanding of the advertising ecosystem, one should understand a little about how ad decisioning works. An understanding of this is critical to your startup because it will frame how third parties will think about working with you to advertise your products on a performance basis. Similarly, this is a good representation of how one set of players in the market leverage math to create arbitrage value buying ad space. Conceptually, this is no different than what we want to do - use technology to identify and value various advertising opportunities.

When an ad request goes to an ad network or ad server, how does it decide what ad to serve? This is increasingly referred to as the science of computational advertising - finding the best match between a user in a context and a suitable ad. This can vary from network to network or server to server, but I want to walk through one hypothetical answer to inform your understanding of advertising. We can use a mathematical representation of a scheduling process to see how an ad server might optimize campaign delivery for a network.

Let's start with some thoughts about optimization in general: Optimization can be defined as a set of choices to maximize some objective function subject to constraints.

If I gave you a piece of paper and told you to make the largest box you could build out of it, that would be an example of a simple optimization challenge.

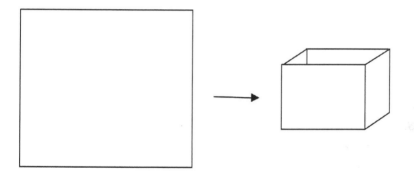

Every optimization challenge has constraints. In this example, a glaring constraint is the size of the paper. You can make a bigger box if you have a bigger piece of paper. Constraining the size of the piece of paper limits the volume the box can have, but we can use math to determine the optimal box shape.

Some examples of constraints in advertising might be:
- There is only so much budget for a given campaign
- There are a limited number of impressions in Maryland

- The advertiser only wants to show the ad to a given consumer a certain number of times per day

Walking through an example is easy and illuminating. For this example, we will pretend we are an ad network. We have mentioned networks before, but let's take a moment to better understand them: Ad networks are very common businesses to find in the advertising ecosystem and are not dissimilar in paradigm from our approach to the problem of digital advertising. They are arbitrageurs; they buy inventory from publishers that struggle to sell their ad space, re-package it, and then re-sell it to advertisers. Many of them, such as the well-known Google AdSense network sell their ads on a performance basis. It is vitally important to a performance-based ad network to show the best performing ads on a given piece of inventory in order to maximize their revenue. In this way, their laser focus on optimizing performance mirrors our own value system.

Let's imagine that we represent an ad network that has two advertisers and two publishers. In many respects, this is similar to our situation as a start-up marketing a product. The two advertisers could be two different creative messages. The two publishers could be any two different things that we are buying; it could be two different targeting mechanisms on the same site or two different pieces of inventory entirely. They are discreet things we can get access to.

For this example, these are performance advertisers so the ad network only gets paid when someone clicks and we have learned that the likelihood that a consumer clicks varies from one site to the next. Fortunately, we have determined through testing already the expected revenue for each advertiser/site combination and we can represent this as a graph:

Revenue	Site	
Advertiser	Site X	Site Y
Advertiser A	$5.00	$2.00
Advertiser B	$10.00	$6.00

Let's think about what advertiser we would want to run on each site. If there were no constraints, the most effective scheduling for this network is to simply run Advertiser B 100% on both sites. This generates $16.00 in revenue.

Revenue	Site		Ad Revenue
Advertiser	Site X	Site Y	
Advertiser A	$5.00	$2.00	$-
Advertiser B	$10.00	$6.00	$16.00
			$16.00
Weights	Site		
Advertiser	Site X	Site Y	
Advertiser A	0%	0%	
Advertiser B	100%	100%	
Site Weights	100%	100%	
Site Revenue	$10.00	$6.00	

That was easy. Without any constraints, network optimization simply consists of picking the best ad on each site. Let's add a very realistic complication: The maximum amount that Advertiser B will spend is $6.00.

Revenue	Site		Ad Revenue
Advertiser	Site X	Site Y	
Advertiser A	$5.00	$2.00	$5.00
Advertiser B	$10.00	$6.00	$6.00
			$11.00
Weights	Site		
Advertiser	Site X	Site Y	
Advertiser A	100%	0%	
Advertiser B	0%	100%	
Site Weights	100%	100%	
Site Revenue	$5.00	$6.00	

That was a bummer. A budget constraint like that can significantly de-optimize the network. Budget constraints force the system to make tradeoffs based on next-best choices. But at least the math was still easy.

Final step: Now let's add the constraint that Advertiser A wants to run equally on every site they run on. For someone like an advertising network, this might be a fairly common constraint because if the Advertiser wanted to run everything on one site, they could contract directly with that site.

Revenue	Site		Ad Revenue
Advertiser	Site X	Site Y	
Advertiser A	$5.00	$2.00	$4.38
Advertiser B	$10.00	$6.00	$6.00
			$10.38
Weights	Site		
Advertiser	Site X	Site Y	
Advertiser A	62.5%	62.5%	
Advertiser B	37.5%	37.5%	
Site Weights	100%	100%	
Site Revenue	$6.88	$3.50	

Now we can see how adding a cross-cell constraint to a linear program can cause a "poor performing campaign" to show more.

In a real ad network for performance advertising, there is typically some "learning function" that needs to go on. In our example, we had perfect information about how advertisers performed on inventory. In the real world, that must be discovered through testing – a certain amount of inventory must be expended on ads that turn out to not perform at all just to discover that they do not perform. Typically this is an on-going process of discovery with results and value constantly fluctuating.

When Turn, one of the largest ad technology companies in the world today, was founded, its initial value proposition was being "Advertising.com for the long tail". They offered a self-service platform that allowed people to buy on a CPA basis. While initially compelling to advertisers, industry insiders (correctly) surmised that this initial model was doomed to fail because the learning costs were simply too high. Without negotiating the value of a CPA event, advertisers could pick very low prices for events that were unlikely. The result was a significant learning cost to Turn to identify pockets of high-performing inventory and little chance to recoup those costs because the pockets were likely too small. At Advertising.com, if we found a CPA campaign that we thought likely to be successful (and we were picky), it typically cost us around $10,000 to test that campaign and determine if it would really work on our network. Turn could not afford to spend that much money for each small advertiser that joined its network.

Also, our model is very simple in that we assumed advertiser performance was only affected by the sites. A model will only be as effective as its reflection of the reality of the business. To the extent that other factors affect the performance of the campaign, their impact on the network must be taken into account.[13]

Let me give you one example of how constraints can cause counter-intuitive results. I was recently running a mobile advertising campaign for a very large brand. That brand had two campaigns running with two distinct targeting mechanisms. In one, they targeted ads to people that were very close to their store. In the other, they ran ads targeted to pretty much anyone. They essentially split their budgets equally between the two. At the end of the campaign, they had higher click through rates for the latter flight then the former and they were confounded. They confronted me: "You showed us so much research indicating that proximity would generate higher CTRs!" My rejoinder was that this was

13. Does an ad impression from a user in India perform differently than a user in the United States? Usually it does. In fact, generally speaking United States user impressions must subsidize all of the foreign traffic a publisher gets because foreign traffic is difficult to monetize effectively.

true, but they failed to consider the constraints generated by their targeting.

There are very few impressions proximate to their store. The campaign essentially consumed all of them. There were many, many impressions available not proximate to the store. The result was, being unconstrained by the proximity requirement, we were able to prune large portions of poor performing inventory (for example, inventory that was on unrelated content). This drove up the performance of the open budget. This optimization was not possible on the campaign with the proximity requirement due to the neediness of the campaign. However, when you compared the CTRs of the two campaigns for any given piece of inventory, you saw higher CTRs on the proximate campaign. So while proximate impressions outperformed more physically distant impressions, the difference was that the poorest performing inventory had been optimized out in the open campaign.

This drives home how over-constraining a campaign up-front can result in an inability to optimize the campaign as performance data is generated, limiting the ability to improve the campaign. If you end up working with a network, you should appreciate this: If you give them very specific targeting parameters, all they can do is deliver that audience. If you give them loose targeting parameters, then they can optimize.

Supply/Demand Imbalance

Remnant vs. Premium

Besides the ability to buy on a performance basis and have real-time detail about how something performs, there is another aspect of digital marketing that has had a powerful impact on the nature of advertising: the imbalance of supply and demand in the market.

To truly understand the implications of supply/demand imbalance, you need to understand how publishers segment their inventory and how their perspective on inventory is dramatically different than advertisers.

This understanding is important because we can use it to our advantage. It also makes clear what opportunities are available, who will want to work with us to execute our master plan for intergalactic domination, and who will be part of the stodgy "old-school" that tries to hold us back!

Publishers conceptually segment their inventory into "premium" and "remnant". Premium is what the publisher can sell themselves. This means that in many respects, there is nothing premium about premium except that, generally, people pay a premium to get access to it. The sole exception to this rule is that many publishers have inventory that they only sell on a premium basis, such as sponsorship or native ad units.

Remnant is what they cannot sell and liquidate using SSPs, exchanges, third party networks or some other system. But remnant is a publisher concept. Advertisers do not buy "remnant". They buy cheap, they buy high-frequency, they buy run-of-x (site, section, some other thing). They trade some modicum of control and the ability to complain for prices that are frequently one-tenth of the going rate.

Publishers would imply that advertisers are choosing between their "premium" and "remnant" inventory, but this is typically a publisher conceit. Advertisers are actually looking to make choices between better impressions and worse impressions for their specific purposes and those impressions are scattered in between the premium and remnant inventory. The first several impressions of a unique tend to perform better. Does buying premium get you that? Maybe? Many publishers don't sell frequency caps as part of their standard IOs. Of course, frequency caps are a tiny part of the optimization equation.

There is also an aspect of user locale that plays into the value proposition associated with inventory. Adobe reported that non-US traffic was worth 70% less than US traffic on a CPM basis.[30] Here is some data from 3Q2011 and 4Q2010 published by Google:

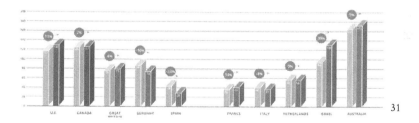

31

These are the countries that have high CPMs. The takeaway is that while huge volumes of traffic to almost any web site are from places like India and China, today those impressions have almost no value. Many advertisers neglect to confine their targeting to US-only inventory, but for most advertisers, this is necessary to achieve strong post click conversion activities.

The Race To The Bottom

Publishers are in the midst of a race to the bottom. They feel tremendous pressure to increase revenue, particularly as "print dollars are replaced with digital dimes". The growth of digital revenue is not replacing print dollars 1:1 as digital ad revenue goes to new sources (primarily Google). While there is very little they can typically do to increase their own sales, an easy way to generate additional revenue is send some more impressions to real time bidded exchanges. To the typical publisher, this seems simple and expedient. They think, "I am getting $0.50 for every 1,000 impressions I send to this RTB exchange. If I found another 10,000,000 impressions per day, that is $5,000 per day ($150,000 per month). Maybe all they need to do is add one more ad unit to their page to get them there.

In the short term, it increases revenue. But in the long term, it is a prisoner's dilemma. In a vacuum, if a publisher adds a new ad to a page and creates additional monetization for themselves, they throw all those impressions into their remnant monetization and generate incremental revenue. Unfortunately, every publisher thinks that. And generally speaking, the amount of buyers in the RTB exchange is fixed. So when everyone adds an incremental ad unit to the page, the net payout for each ad goes down and over time, the CPM simply settles at a lower level.

This is particularly true because typically the new inventory being created is low quality. It might be "below the fold" (a consumer must scroll down to see it). It might be small. It might simply be the tenth ad on the page. All of these things make an ad less valuable. And as more and more ads appear on the page, even the high quality ad inventory becomes less valuable.

Unfortunately, the people most likely to flood an exchange with low quality inventory are not the best actors. Frankly, they are the worst. The lowest quality, worst kind of inventory. And as they flood the world of programmatic buying, causing CPMs to fall for everyone, the response of the best actors is frequently to respond in kind. As their CPMs decline, adding inventory is the only way to maintain or grow revenue.

This means most inventory is bad and getting worse. This is why we believe in paying for performance. Because supply is growing rapidly, performance prices should decline as well (albeit not as fast as CPM prices, but more in-line with actual performance), so the value opportunity increases. Even premium publishers are adding poor performing inventory units.

In the mobile space, we started out being strong believers in having one ad per page. Soon, that ad unit was an "adhesive" unit that stuck to the top or bottom of the page. Then publishers wanted to ad in-line ads in addition to the adhesive unit. Publishers always want to add more ad units. These impact the value proposition to advertisers, but the marginal revenue is too important to publishers.

Viewable Impressions

Viewable Impressions is the advertiser's response to the publisher race to the bottom. Advertisers are increasingly deploying technology that allows them to tell if the advertisement has been seen on the consumers screen. Most industry analysts believe this will be very powerful as they suspect that more than 50% of the inventory available in exchanges today are impressions that are never actually seen by a consumer.[32] (54% according to a recent comScore study.[33])

While viewable impression standards exist for display advertising (The IAB designates a viewable ad as any impression where at least half of the ad is viewable on the page for one second or more.), they will soon be equally relevant and important for mobile, tablet, and cross-screen marketing. Personally, I have seen many instances of mobile applications polling ad networks for ads in the background of the application and generating false click events. I suspect that there will be much more of this in the future as the mobile wild west continues to unfold.

The MRC (Media Ratings Council) recently blessed the viewable ads initiative as finally making digital advertising valuable, but even members of the council such as Nielsen acknowledge[34] that the 11 different "approved" viewable metric measurers all generate completely different numbers because their approaches are widely variable.

Theoretically, if viewable impressions are effective, they will weed out many low quality publishers, increase the value of top publisher inventory, and cause CPMs to rise for quality publishers. Google recently introduced new options in their ad exchange that allow advertisers to only pay for viewable impressions.

Performance advertisers are particularly excited about the advent of viewable impressions. To the extent that view-through impressions are seen as a viable pricing or attribution mechanism, performance networks that may have been buying very low price, very low quality unviewed impressions to "cookie bomb" and receive attribution credit for a later converter that was not even motivated by their ad, an advertiser can weed out these networks and this inventory.

Unfortunately, in the early going of marketing, paying the fees to third party services to verify viewability probably is not worth it. You are better served simply making sure that you are only paying people when you make money. If you are getting a dollar every time you spend fifty cents, even if some of that fifty cents wasn't really earned, it still provides a framework for scale. As the little guy, we should try to rely on the big actors in the market to clean up some of this rather than taking on this burden ourselves.

The good news for you is that the medium term outlook for viewability for everyone is good. In the short term, brand advertisers and large agencies - the most valuable advertisers in the market - will be the people investing in viewability. This will drastically reduce the CPMs paid for non-viewable inventory, hopefully driving it out of the market. Free riders will benefit as quality publishers will re-shape their user experience to increase viewability and quality of inventory. This improves the experience for all advertisers.

Ad Blockers

Ad blocking software has been around for many years but two events have occurred that have caused the issue of ad blocking to be highlighted recently.

First, ad blocking on mobile has become a thing. iOS 9 allowed ad blockers to activate on mobile devices and several of these products quickly jumped to the most popular products sold in the Apple App Store.

Second, possibly fueled by the widespread awareness of mobile ad blockers engendered by the App Store marketing power, ad blockers on desktop also grew dramatically - as much as 48% year over year[35].

The most popular product, Ad Block Plus, has a pay-to-play whitelist business model. That is, you can pay them to have your ads show regardless of whether the consumer is using their ad blocker. Microsoft, Google and others are rumored to be among the people that have already paid to play.

If you think that sounds insanely hypocritical of the vendor, you are not alone.

Unfortunately for publishers, there is little that can be done about this, but I think the key underlying concepts that we see in the market are closely related to a consumer's desire to block ads:

- Poor creative experiences
- Too many pixels, too much ad tech, too much page bloat
- Race to the bottom with more and more ads on pages

While many publishers are working on approaches such as more native advertising to work around ad blockers, I suspect the real answer here over the long term is to continue to work to create meaningful experiences for consumers, emphasize viewable impressions, and recognize that this will exert a pressure on the market that will limit supply over time.

Scaling Acquisition

We are at the final step of our journey to use digital advertising to enable lean startups. Our objective now is to develop marketing systems that, once created, can take advantage of this advertising ecosystem to scale from driving dozens of new customers to thousands with the only additional input being more marketing expenses.

The goal is to be as lean in our approach to digital advertising as we have been with the rest of our startup. We want to test advertising techniques, validate their effectiveness as quickly as we can, scale up the ones that are working and shut down the ones that are not. Unfortunately, there are so many things to test that we cannot test them all.

The good news is that we have the benefits of knowledge and experience to guide the selection and prioritization of key strategies. Hence, we can break traditional and non-traditional marketing activities into activities that, at a high level, tend to be effective for lean advertising strategies and those that do not.

Where Do I Start?

The ABCs of Google

There is a reason Google has grown to be one of the largest, most profitable companies in the world. First, it is the most powerful tool for large scale lower funnel advertising ever. Second, it is a versatile tool for testing a variety of keys to your marketing success in every aspect of your strategy.

I want to talk about Google in two contexts. First, how to use search to acquire customers in the big picture scheme of things.

Second, how to use it to test and evaluate your products for driving to product.

Search Marketing is the easiest, most effective marketing available in the digital world. It is the starting point for every business that advertises online because everyone uses Google and has seen their ads. And it is not just the starting point because people have heard of Google: It is the starting point because it works.

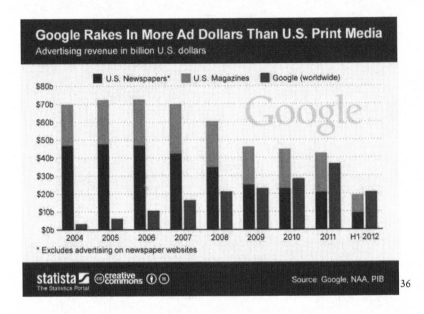

Google is the primary beneficiary of search marketing today. As the above graph indicates, Google is now one of the biggest generators of ad revenue in the world, outpacing the entire magazine and newspaper industry combined.

If you are selling a physical good, Google will be an important part of your market mix as your business grows. Being good at working with Google is important. There is no better location for finding directed intention on the Internet.

Search Engine Marketing, or SEM, is buying keywords to display ads on search engines. Selling those ad slots is how Google makes most of their money. Search marketing is a very effective way to reach consumers at many points in the marketing funnel life cycle. If someone searches for "big screen TV", they are probably considering buying a big screen TV. If we bought that keyword on Google and the first search result listing was your advertisement for big screen TVs that you are selling, the odds of actually closing a sale are high. Contrast that with a television ad on the television show "CSI" – a small, small portion of the people you reach are in the market for buying a big screen TV. In fact, many of them are probably watching the show on a big screen already – they will not be in market again for years and years. Many of the eyeballs that saw that ad have a value of zero. The power of search marketing is that the keyword targeting enables you to reach only customers that are in-market.

Suppose you do a web search for a pizza shop in Santa Fe, New Mexico, an advertiser can bid to "own" that keyword. At any given moment, she wants to reach people that are interested in getting a pizza in Santa Fe. The moment they do a search, that ad appears – it might be the exact ad the consumer is looking for. Consumer then pays for that click. For Google, the consumer clicking that ad is a virtual "vote". By demonstrating your relevance to that query by being the recipient of the consumer click, Google becomes more likely to show that ad again at a similar search query.

With search engines, advertisers typically bid on keyword phrases relevant to their target market. By convention, the ads on these search engines are priced on a cost-per-click basis and are formatted to be similar to the results of a search engine query result. For instance, if I'm trying to sell flowers, I can designate to Google that I want to show up when people search for things like

"Washington DC flower shop", "Mothers day flowers in Washington DC" or "Flower Delivery in Washington DC". The advertiser provides a list of the terms they want to target and the CPC bids they are willing to pay for each of them.

When the ad is displayed, Google uses the frequency of consumers clicking on the ad as a virtual poll to judge the relevance of the ad. Frequent clicks demonstrate well-targeted, relevant ads. As Google is self-interested in generating clicks, they use the quality score - a concept that captures how likely a consumer is to click an advertisement - and the CPC bid of the advertiser to show the ads that are most likely to yield revenue for Google.

Bidding can get extremely complicated the further you get into SEM: Negative keywords (don't target people who mention "anchovy pizza" - we don't have that), keyword expansion, match types, and many aspects of bidding, and many other aspects of search marketing, but at a high level the important thing is this: The first step to Google is to start small in all things. For example, the starting point in customer acquisition in buying clicks on Google is to spend $250 to test drive a few hundred clicks and see what happens. Don't spend more than twenty or thirty dollars per day and don't pay more than $2.00 or $2.50 per click. You will need a few conversions for any given keyword to accurately identify the performance for that keyword, so start with a small, targeted list of five to ten terms and slowly expand out from there.

That sounds easy enough, but cheap clicks aren't always easy to find. You are a start-up. You should assume that the popular, highly effective keywords with tremendous volume have high bid prices already. Terms like "flight to Las Vegas" are bid on very aggressively by companies in the travel space today. As a very early stage company, the odds that you can go after the large volume, high performance terms that will work most effectively for your business in the long term, having high volume while driving high conversion rates, are low. You need to drill down into the niche. Don't start with big "head" terms, identify very granular terms. If you sell Wolverine figurines, don't try to buy the term "wolverine", buy "x-men action figures wolverine". You need to drill down all the way to the bottom to find where you will be able to get high performance searches at reasonable prices because you are not able to bid aggressively for traffic yet.

Why can you not bid aggressively? This is because you have not yet optimized your conversion paths for winning. To maximize the amount you can bid on these terms, you have to be incredibly efficient at turning visitors into money. The first bursts of traffic you buy on Google will not be focused on generating maximum revenue, but generating maximum learnings. You have to learn how to make revenue and that starts with the "ABC's" of digital advertising: "Always be conversion optimizing"[14].

The key to this test is that you are testing what happens when people get to your site. You must think about what parts of your sites conversion path need to be tested and test them. Don't start small with things like button colors – that will only lead you to a local maxima. Think big and test big out of the gate. But the focus of that first 100 visitors, 200 visitors, 500 visitors is about understanding the bottlenecks to your conversion flow, testing alternatives, and getting after that specific aspect of your digital marketing platform.

Google also has related products such as Google PLA, Google's product listing service. Google PLA recently supplanted Google's comparison shopping service as a new paid listing product search. Because it is relatively new, this is a channel that offers a lot of op-

---

14. OK, that was kind of brutal. I apologize for that. You deserve better.

portunities to retailers of goods. Most of the product listings uploaded to PLA today are not optimized for search, which means that some people are seeing very strong performance simply by preparing their product listings to better represent their products as standalone ads.

The Next Big Thing

While Google is the best place to start, you may find that it simply doesn't work for you. The problem is that everyone is there already. Prices are high because they have the demand.

One of the most important things for you to do as you embark on driving large scale demand and testing is to try the new, new thing. The places where there will be the most broad discrepancies between supply and demand are places that just started to build their own advertising platform.

Today that means places like Twitter and Instagram. Tomorrow it might be Pinterest and Snapchat. The early bird here gets the worm. Virtually all of these platforms envision building a bidded performance marketplace such as Google. If you hear of a large audience platform rolling out a bidded cost per click market, I urge you to test it and test it quickly. Typically, early on in a market's lifecycle, it will have higher CTRs as the audience is not numb to advertising messages yet. This gives you the chance to buy low price, high performance clicks. Do so!

Unlike Google, where it is extraordinarily difficult to find nickel clicks, you should be able to buy large volumes of traffic for less than $0.25. Here, effective analytics will be important because without the powerful intent signals of Google keywords, you could end up with a lot of traffic that performs poorly on the backend, but if you can buy clicks for half the price of Google, the conversion rate could be half of Google's and you could still find value.

You will note when you start working on these projects that the other parties you will find here will be hard core affiliate arbitrageurs. This means you are doing it right. Much like you, they are looking for seams of high performance where they can pour money in and generate positive economic outcomes.

Now, note that I did not mention markets that aren't performance-related. If someone is rolling out a "new native ad platform" or something like that, that is great for them, but we pay for performance. Many publishers and networks will generate a stream of new targeting mechanisms and creative formats, but if they aren't performance-based systems that we can inexpensively test, they are not of interest to us.

Pipe Dreams & Other Things

Affiliate Marketing

Affiliate marketing sounds like a brilliant strategy for any company: third parties rise up and sell your product and they only get paid when they make a sale. Unfortunately, affiliate marketing is much like nearly every business development project I have been involved in. The universal truth of business development and partnerships is this: You get out of it what you put into it. Unfortunately, as a lean startup, your whole strategy revolves around putting less into things than you get out. Even if you were eager to invest significantly, you have precious little to offer.

From an infrastructure perspective, you can easily plug and play affiliate using a system like Commission Junction, but unfortunately, a one-size fits all affiliate model, and a model where you are competing for affiliates with thousands of other affiliate offerers is a difficult environment for your tiny, lean brand to succeed in.

Setting that aside, you have two problems inherent to the lean startup that will prevent affiliate from being successful for you. First, your marketing potential sucks for a professional affiliate: Professional affiliate marketers have several built-in assumptions for things that they think will convert well. One is the market; if you are selling a weight-loss product, a penis-enlarging product, and these kind of snake oil health and beauty products, there is a tremendous market of dedicated affiliate arbitrageurs interested in jumping on your product. There arbitrageurs are not available to you if you are not in this market.

The second thing affiliate marketers look for is a great brand. Absent a product that people will buy irrespective of brand (e.g. weight-loss), a brand can make or break a product. It is easier for an affiliate marketer to sell Coca-Cola than it is to sell Bob's Root Beer.

The third factor in affiliate marketers minds is related and it is air cover. Affiliate marketers objectives are not to make your life easier. They want to hear about how you make their life easier. Big brands offer the allure of TV advertising and other marketing activities that the affiliate marketer can ride the coattails of to poach bottom of the funnel conversions. Affiliate marketers would rather feel like they are sitting at the bottom of the funnel stealing conversions than creating top of the funnel demand. Knowing that big brands will create demand for them makes their job easier and makes it more alluring.

The second problem you have with affiliate marketing is your price point. Your price point is not interesting because your conversion path is not optimized. As we discussed, people like University of Phoenix are so strong at conversions that they can require fairly simple actions by the affiliate marketer and pay extremely high payouts for those actions. Your conversion path is not as simple (Simple is three or four field forms and no payment information required).

Consider the Coca-Cola example earlier. Not only are conversions simpler for Coca-Cola because they are one of the biggest brands in the world, they have the best of both worlds: They can probably pay out more and affiliate marketers are more interested in pushing their product. Hence affiliate tends to be a winner-take-most kind of market. If you can't attract a lot of affiliates, you will not attract any affiliates. When it works, every affiliate dives in.

This is similar to hiring commission-only sales people. I have met many start-ups that have a vision that they will be able to hire sales people on a commission-only basis and that this will successfully propel their business toward some objective, but in all my time I have found that the only sales people attracted to the opportunity to work for commission-only at a high risk start-up are the least employable, least successful sales people, likely to jump ship the moment the moment an alternative comes along.

The only way to get ahead of this game as a small company is offer an exorbitant amount for a conversion. This will incent the affiliate marketer to overcome their aversion to working with brands that do not provide air cover and do not have simple conversion paths. Unfortunately, there is no way to make this work. Affiliates in this situation will create your entire marketing strategy. Unfortunately, without a high LCV to prop it up, their ability to execute on all of the things we are outlining here is no better than yours.

CPM Banners

Promise me, promise me, promise me, you will not call ESPN.com and just buy a bunch of banners. For that matter, you will not go into Google AdWords and pay on a per impression basis for inventory on sites. The first time you pay for impressions without having some learnings about the amount of revenue they will generate for you, I will come to your house and revoke your lean card. I don't care how relevant it sounds, it is no way to make a living.

The average CTR in display media today is below 0.1%. That means that the CPC you will pay for media on a CPM basis will typically be a multiple of the CPM. If, by some miracle, you are able to buy quality inventory for $0.50 CPMs, you will still end up spending nearly $1.00 per click in most situations and your cost per conversion will probably be more than $100.00 per conversion.

If you pay $4.50 CPMs (The minimum for ESPN's self-service ad tool), you will pay approximately $8.00 per click for unfrequency capped ad serving. This will turn into $1000.00 per conversion fairly quickly. This is not the lean way. Lean people pay for results. We will look for people already close to the bottom of the funnel with tricky tactics. We won't run Super Bowl ads with our VC money and we won't pay CPMs for inventory when Google will sell us lower CPC inventory for people who have high intent and likelihood to convert on a per click basis.

Tactics For Advertising Businesses

As a sidebar, we should discuss the challenges associated with generating traffic to your site if your plan is to build a site funded by advertising.

In short, you cannot pay for traffic. If you look at the success of content farms such as Demand Media a few years ago, they generated traffic by optimizing for Google. Google showed them as a high result for every query, so they captured traffic with aggressive SEO strategies. Modern day content farms such as Buzzfeed are not particularly different. They have optimized their content for sharing on social networks and have built a strong viral loop.

The other approach to creating effective sites fueled by advertising is to create a page flywheel. Sites like Wikipedia, Twitter and Facebook (social networks) rely on users to recruit other users by creating content that those users are interested in consuming. This strategy allows a very small core team to provide a platform for users to create the content that drives page views. This is effective, but much like a flywheel, overcoming initial inertia is very difficult. The key to this model is that customer acquisition centers on creating content creators, not attracting content consumers. The conventional wisdom of these businesses is that there is a power law where 10% of the visitors create content, while 90% consume content. Attracting that 10% is vital.

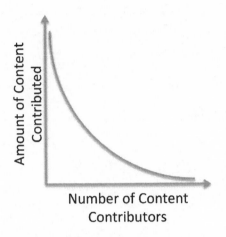

Paying for traffic is extremely difficult to make work in a situation such as this because the value of a visit is so low. Imagine a world where you are selling 40% of your inventory direct for $4.00 and 60% as remnant inventory to ad networks for $0.40. This blends to an eRPM of $1.84. If you are buying traffic even at a CPC of $0.10 (e.g. Incredibly cheaply) that means you are paying $0.10 for a visitor. For 1,000 visitors (generating $1.84 in revenue on the first ad view), you must pay $100.00. Even if you have low bounce rates, several ads on a page and people consume several pages per visit, the economics of buying traffic to be sold are unsustainable.

In the flywheel model, you may find that a content creator is worth $10.00 to the business, so this more complex example of a conversion can allow you to create a business model that is workable, but recognize that the focus is not on attracting traffic that you monetize with ads – that model is never economically viable. The focus is advertising to acquire content creators, which is a different business. This is still a difficult conversion. It may be easier to optimize your conversion path to turn consumers into creators than find pockets of creators you can attract.

Effective Lean Direct Response

Deep Dive on AdWords

Hail the almighty power of Google. Google AdWords is the largest CPC network on the Internet and is also the best performing. They have better technology, better inventory (thanks to SERP pages) and more insight into what is working and not working with minimal expense. That means that the starting point for almost every direct marketer is Google.

The good news is that it is easy to get started with AdWords. The bad news is that AdWords has almost infinite complexity and there are giant companies that have hundreds of people focused on nothing but being good at AdWords. So becoming an expert is hard, but it is worth working very hard to be great at buying AdWords.

There are entire web sites and books devoted to buying AdWords and you should go find those, but I will share a few high-level tips if you want to dive in and buy a hundred clicks to start testing.

- Google offers two kinds of inventory; search engine results pages (SERPs) and content marketing. Content marketing is when they find "contextually relevant pages" provided by third parties. This is when AdWords ads appear on things like blogs or content farms. You should start testing exclusively on SERPs and make sure that your test is turned off for content marketing. Those two inventory sources perform very differently and you will NEVER want to conflate the two. If you want to test content marketing, you create a separate campaign targeted to content marketing and restricted from showing on SERPs. You will have to bid more for SERPs, but performance will be significantly higher. Always, always, for as long as you work with Google, have separate ad groups for SERPs and non-SERP inventory. Non-SERPs have cheaper clicks (because smart people don't buy them) but lower conversion rates. Segmenting them is critical to aligning your costs with revenue generation.

- Start with very few keywords. Start with five to ten keywords and start with them set on exact match. You do not want Google to start trying to pick other keywords that it thinks are similar. You want to know what keywords work and what keywords don't. As data comes in, turn off keywords that don't work well on the backend and do keyword expands (adding more related keywords) around terms that perform well. Once again, the experts are doing this so if you don't, Google will run your ads on keywords with high click-through rates and poor conversion rates because the experts are outbidding you on strong converting terms and under-bidding you on the poor converting terms.

- People talk about power terms all the time. These generate an outsize portion of your traffic. Certain keywords have less demand or are more centric to your target market – these perform better. There might be a few keywords that are so effective and efficient on search that they can get you two customers per day for a nickel but there is not enough volume to get more. Brainstorm new terms (or in industry parlance "do a keyword expand") to try to identify related terms. There may be more volume on those terms or sites but you are being outbid. You should test different price points to see how it affects your position on the page, volume and backend performance.

- Test many creatives and messages. Always be testing creatives. Google uses a multi-arm bandit algorithm, so if you load many creatives into an Ad Group, it will test them all, then use the one that performs the best for most of your ads. If you want to make sure you are squeezing all you can out of an Ad Group, delete a creative after 30 clicks if it is performing poorly, but you should replace it with a new test to continue learning.

- Google Analytics needs to be set up properly. One of the best things about AdWords is that it is easy to integrate with Google's Analytics product to track conversions down to the creative and keyword level.

This is why LCV is so important – higher value allows you to get more customers and grow faster. As you tap out the volume available in your power terms you have two choices; Raise your bid to get more clicks associated with the term or bid on more terms looking for pockets of low cost clicks that perform well. This process continues in an upward spiral of rising bids and keyword expansion until you have exhausted the ability to acquire conversions below your LCV.

As you scale up, there are other processes that should be going on simultaneously. Optimizing and rotating creatives (burnout happens) and optimizing page position (3rd position might perform better on backend)

Doing this by hand is fine to start, but there are many tools to help you do this. They get better the more you spend – Marin and Efficient Frontier are some of the market leaders, but you will need to be spending hundreds of thousands of dollars per year before it makes sense to use these.

AdWords is also a powerful tool for testing messages on the creative side and you should definitely be thinking of innovative ways to use the power of reaching people on SERPs pages to test ideas related to messages. One well-known example of this is that Tim Ferriss, author of the popular "Four Hour Work Week" book, used AdWords to test different ideas for titles for his first book. When he saw that the click-through rate for "Four Hour Work Week" was far higher than any of his other title ideas, he knew he had found the title for his book. People have done the same thing to test company names, feature resonance with markets, and even titles for blog posts.

Generally speaking, whether you are using Google or the "New, New Thing" or some other approach, all of these concepts are important and relevant aspects of the methodology to building a scalable revenue engine.

Retargeting

We have talked about the power of retargeting. The ability to reach out and re-engage people that have visited your site and expressed a connection with your brand is unprecedented in advertising.

Once we have gone beyond using AdWords for testing keywords and we are ready to start driving traffic, it would be remiss
to not take advantage of the power of retargeting. Fortunately,
AdWords content marketing is the largest ad network in the
world and it supports retargeting. You can set up a campaign that
retarget right from within the AdWords interface.

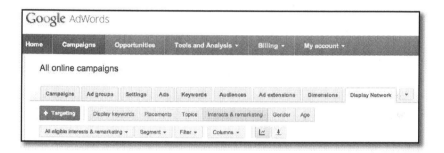

That means that we have a single tool to manage all of these
campaigns, our analytics will be rolled into Google Analytics, and
you are already an AdWords guru, so using this tool is easy (although if you are a guru, you are using the Google AdWords editor
tool rather than the web UI). Further, this will continue to help
you focus your learning on a single analytic tool and single campaign management interface. This is consistent with our 80/20
goals. We want to know our tools cold and be close to the iron,
but we want to spend time working on our business, not mucking
with a bunch of tools. It's better to be really deep on these two
tools than have a shallow understanding of many tools.

Also, because Google will let you remarket on a CPC basis, you
should be able to bid a fairly low bid because you can expect your
remarketed ads to have high click-through rates and good quality.

Finally, remarketing will be a relatively small line item: Remember, remarketing is limited to showing ads to people that you

have already driven to your site. If you are showing hundreds of thousands of ads per day on your remarketing campaign, then you are already winning the Internet.

The one other nuance that you should add to your remarketing strategy is testing frequency and timing. I would suggest placing several pixels on your pages and targeting them with various windows. One pixel might be for a group that has visited in the last seven days. Another might be for a group that has visited between eight and fourteen days ago. A final group might be for people that have visited between fifteen and thirty days ago. While the product you are selling may have different characteristics, generally speaking most retargeting is most effective in the hours and days right after they visit. Hence you will want to have a very loose frequency cap for the visitors that relatively recently visited you, with a tighter cap on people that did not visit as recently.

As these campaigns run, you can then segment out performance by cookie age and adjust your frequency to reflect the performance of varying segments. If a segment is performing extraordinarily well, then loosen the cap and try to get more volume around that time period. If a segment is performing poorly, tighten the frequency cap to improve performance. Remember, tighter caps will improve performance but constrain delivery. Finding a balance is the best way to optimize revenue.

If you find that this is working effectively, as the business scales up, it may behoove you to partner with companies such as Criteo. Criteo is a special remarketing network for retailers where they track the products people look at on a retail site and then dynamically build retargeted creatives featuring those products. This is so effective that Criteo is able to charge on a CPC basis and take on the risk of delivery.

Facebook, Twitter & Social Networks

Many people think of Facebook as something to try if you have the kind of product that appeals to "certain kinds of people" or might play well in some kind of social context. Not true. Facebook has excellent tools for all kinds of advertisers and has invested heavily in offering a range of mechanisms. With the range of targeting mechanisms, optimizations, and creative types that they offer, you would be remiss to not invest extensively in working on Facebook advertising.

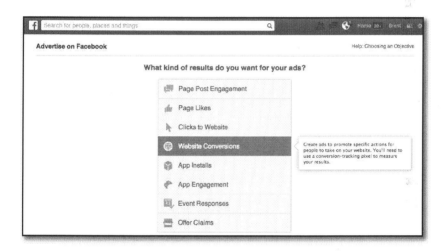

Like Google, the default for Facebook is to combine many different kinds of targeting mechanisms. You should carefully segment out things like advertising in the News Feed (far more effective than the right side bar), Sponsored Stories, and other ad and targeting mechanisms to understand the conversion impact of each of those tools and know where you want to invest your bidding.

Facebook has also introduced a concept called "custom audiences". Custom audiences will perform well for you and is "must do" advertising. Similar to remarketing, it allows you to upload lists of email addresses and target them. By building out an email list and targeting those users that have already expressed interest, this is a very effective path to high engagement.

One common tactic among Facebook power advertisers is to use the Facebook "Offers" creative to offer a free product in exchange for an email address, then build custom audiences to upsell more valuable products. Unfortunately, Facebook today requires a minimum number of page fans (currently 500) to enable this feature.

Facebook has free tools such as the Power Editor that will make managing and segmenting campaigns more straightforward.

Twitter is earlier on it's lifecycle as an advertising platform and it's products are much less mature today. However, I believe that in these early days, there are great opportunities to create leverage in new ad platforms with scale. As Facebook was just taking off, Zynga virtually built it's entire business using the Facebook platform. It is likely that cracking the code on Twitter will create a similar opportunity for some lucky start-up. Similarly, Pinterest, LinkedIn, Tumblr, and Instagram all seem like large social networks that could create interesting marketing opportunities for the right company. Having said that, I would never pay on a CPM basis for any of this inventory.

One social network I think is particular intriguing for early stage businesses is Kickstarter. While many people don't think of Kickstarter as a social network, they are missing the point: Kickstarter has created a site that aggregates early adopters. The people visiting Kickstarter are people that like to try new things. Thinking about ways to offer interesting Kickstarter projects as a way of engaging that community is a very effective viral marketing technique and marketing tool to reach the early adopter community.

Email Marketing 101

You need to be building an email list. There are great tools for managing an email list. MailChimp is a popular tool that is free for the first 2,000 email addresses (Aweber is another common tool). Sending either mass or, preferably, targeted and personalized emails to your existing user base to convert them into a paying customer or entice repeat purchases is incredibly effective. This is probably the most cost-effective and under-utilized tactic for most startups.

You should expect that one of every five emails you send will be opened. If it is less, you have work to do. If it is more, then you are winning the Internet.

Besides just tracking the emails you get, you should add a sign-up form to your site. 74% of people building email lists use this tactic.[37] You should too.

This list will be used for marketing, for launching new products, and for Facebook custom audiences. There is no shortage of ideas you will have for your list once you start building it.

Building the Asset

Let's talk about where you are driving all this traffic. You are building great conversion paths and thinking about landing pages, but there are aspects of both and their relation to direct marketing, viral effects, and SEO that are worth considering for a moment. That is the value of building assets that your customers want. There are several different kinds of assets you can build and they each have different benefits and value propositions.

When you think about tool sets that you can share with customers and leverage into your business, ideally they have several important attributes:

- They should map to the customer decision-making process
- They should educate prospects
- They should be top of funnel activities that identify and qualify prospects

One example of these kinds of tools are report cards. SEOMoz does a great job of this. The products they sell are tools to improve your SEO. For free, they offer a variety of tools that look at your site and tell you how well you are doing SEO. The classic principle here is the diagnosis is free, but the cure costs money. Then when they are doing their advertising activity, they are advertising their free products. Marketing free products facilitates stronger calls to action and higher click-through rates, accelerating people down SEOMoz's well-honed funnel.

Another example are embeddable widgets and distribution partnerships – I call this "spreading your code". Free services that get distributed and shared by your customers allow you to leverage third parties for marketing activation. Toolbars and sharing widgets on blogs are great examples of this. You can use these marketing models to test calls to action, generate traffic, and improve your SEO, but make sure you don't let distribution of this product distract you from honing your own message and focusing on revenue generating activity.

CPI

Cost-Per-Install (CPI) campaigns for mobile applications are one of the few kinds of real bottom-of-the-funnel CPA campaigns that it is possible for start-ups to buy. Many networks such as Flurry, Millennial Media, Appia, and Fiksu will offer to distribute your mobile application on a CPI basis and typically charge from $0.50 to $4 per install for free apps with broad target markets. This varies depending on the likelihood that a customer will install the app. So it might be on the low end for a casual game that many people are likely to be interested in such as Candy Crush or Angry Birds. It will be on the high end for a niche application. Facebook's in-app marketing program is one of the most effective, driving installs at the low end of these price points.

For the first several years that app stores were in production, it was possible to use CPI campaigns to game the app store rankings. Much like content farmers game Google and Google constantly works to foil their efforts, the app stores are aggressively trying to determine ways to prevent CPI from impacting their popularity rankings. Despite this, it is important to discuss with any ad network their perspective on impacting organic app store rankings and how to structure campaigns for maximum success in this regard.

If you built an app, many of the things I have talked about are true, but some of them are different. SEO is less important because most app discovery occurs in the app store. Conversion and engagement and sharing are vitally important. These are the keys to high LCV and high conversion rates and if you don't execute well on them, you won't be able to drive installs. If you execute well on them, then the world is your oyster.

Free apps like Candy Crush are so well-architected to drive in-app purchases and monetizable behavior that they will pay several dollars to app install networks such as Flurry and Appia to drive installs. This serves two purposes: First, the LCV of these products is so high that it is a profitable action independent of other value. Second, the steady stream of installs preserves their position atop app store ranking lists. This drives a stream of organic downloads that are relatively costless and high margin - improving LCV.

You will want to identify a partner such as HasOffers or Ad-X to help you manage attribution across these networks rather than installing a variety of SDKs (Software Development Kits, the code that one installs to enable this functionality). Of course, if you are working with Flurry and already using Flurry for mobile analytics, you will find that you path is much easier.

If you get an ad tag from Appia and spend some time requesting ads using it, the ads you receive from Appia read like a who's who list of top app store downloads. It is naive to assume that the magic of these apps dominance of the top position is simply a function of brilliant app development. It is happening via tight collaboration with marketing partners.

If you are developing mobile apps, the most important part of your strategy is optimizing your experience to ensure that your LCV is high enough to work with these hard core direct response networks. Paying for actual downloads of the app is considered standard practice for large portions of the industry. The only requirement is that you will have to pay their price.

The price demanded by each of these networks is based on the competitiveness of their internal marketplace (how their ad decisioning works). The less you pay, the more likely, in any given auction, that you will be outbid by the hot app du jour. These apps will tend to run with sizeable budgets because every install they drive creates incremental revenue. Thus, you will not be able to "get the price down" and getting the price down only results in more limited volume for you.

The more you pay, the more volume you will get and there are distinct inflection points where higher payouts will open up pockets of high performing inventory to drive substantial installs.

One key aspect of CPI campaigns to keep in mind is that app stores are generally organized by country and driving US installations is generally far more expensive (and far more valuable) than driving international installs. Much like international display advertising traffic, there are significant differences in cost between countries.

Paid apps tend to have much higher CPI prices because typically they have much smaller markets. I was recently contacted by the tourist bureau of a small Caribbean island and asked about selling their free tourism apps on a CPI basis. It turns out that only about 40,000 people visited the island in any given year. This implies that it would have been extremely difficult to find and target those people effectively. This is an example of an app that is probably inappropriate for CPI marketing. Because it was a free app, the value of the installation was very low, even for the people marketing it, yet the cost of finding those few people intending to visit would have been prohibitive.

Notes

1. http://www.iab.net/adunitportfolio

2.
http://www.iab.net/guidelines/508676/508767/ad_unit/displayri
singstars
3.   http://www.mediabrix.com/wp-
content/uploads/2013/02/MediaBrix_Report_201211.pdf
4.
http://www.iab.net/media/file/IABInternetAdvertisingRevenueR
eportFY2012POSTED.pdf
5.   http://www.zenithoptimedia.com/wp-
content/uploads/2013/12/Adspend-forecasts-December-2013-
executive-summary.pdf
6.
http://www.iab.net/media/file/IABInternetAdvertisingRevenueR
eportFY2012POSTED.pdf
7.   http://www.vantagelocal.com/history-of-online-display-
advertising-2/
8.   http://www.emarketer.com/newsroom/index.php/google-
display-ad-leader/
9.   http://www.emarketer.com/Article/Online-Video-
Advertising-Moves-Front-Center/1009886
10.   http://www.slideshare.net/mediapostlive/borrell-mobile-
insider-summit
11.   http://www.zenithoptimedia.com/wp-
content/uploads/2013/12/Adspend-forecasts-December-2013-
executive-summary.pdf
12.   http://techcrunch.com/2014/04/07/internet-ad-spend-to-
reach-121b-in-2014-23-of-537b-total-ad-spend-ad-tech-gives-
display-a-boost-over-search/

13. http://www.aicpalearning.org/profdev_news.asp?a_id=10273&cat =Enews&uid=&m=

14. http://www.kpcb.com/insights/2013-internet-trends

15. http://www.emarketer.com/Article/Most-Digital-Ad-Growth-Now-Goes-Mobile-Desktop-Growth-Falters/1010458/1

16. http://www.clickz.com/clickz/news/2222543/us-mobile-local-ad-revenue-will-reach-usd58-billion-by-2016

17. http://www.theatlantic.com/magazine/archive/2014/01/the-dark-lord-of-the-internet/355726/2/

18. http://www.alchemyworx.com/2013/research/dma_client_email_study_2013.pdf

19. http://quibb.com/links/4-steps-to-better-retention-with-follow-up-loops/view

20. http://www.emarketer.com/Article/Premium-Publishers-See-Hope-Native-Sponsorships/1010402

21. http://www.slideshare.net/tkawaja/terence-kawajas-iab-networks-and-exchanges-keynote

22. http://adsense.blogspot.com/2010/05/adsense-revenue-share.html

23. http://www.adexchanger.com/online-advertising/why-programmatic-in-house-is-gaining-favor-with-marketers/

24. http://www.businessinsider.com/15-things-you-need-to-know-about-internet-porn-2011-8?op=1

25. http://www.emarketer.com/Article/Programmatic-Ad-Spend-Set-Soar/1010343

26. IDC, October 16, 2013

27. http://www.emarketer.com/Article/Programmatic-Ad-Spend-Set-Soar/1010343

28. https://code.google.com/p/openrtb/

29. http://adexchanger.com/ad-exchange-news/google-is-beta-testing-its-answer-to-header-bidding-called-dfp-first-look/

30. https://blogs.adobe.com/digitalmarketing/digital-marketing/social-media/going-beyond-the-us-in-display/

31. http://static.googleusercontent.com/media/www.google.com/en/us/doubleclick/pdfs/display-business-trends-publisher-edition.pdf

32. http://adage.com/article/digital/viewability-half-online-ads/242026/

33. http://www.comscore.com/Insights/Blog/Viewability_Benchmarks_Show_Many_Ads_Are_Not_In-View_but_Rates_Vary_by_Publisher

34. http://www.adexchanger.com/online-advertising/mrc-standards-are-only-a-starting-point-for-viewability/

35. http://blog.pagefair.com/2015/ad-blocking-report/

36. http://www.statista.com/topics/1001/google/chart/709/google-s-ad-revenue-since-2004/

37. http://www.marketingcharts.com/wp/online/email-list-growth-marketers-rank-their-most-popular-and-effective-tactics-37943/

CHAPTER 12

Things You Can Buy To Buy Customers

Targeting

We now understand all the different formats we have for reaching customers and the mechanics for how they work. Next, lets discuss different types of targeting mechanisms for you to reach specific customers. A large part of this discussion will be to highlight that these things are not new or special! If someone offers you these products, do not be seduced by their magical sounding attributes! These targeting mechanisms are commonplace today.

The reason these things are not generally of interest to you is that few people (aside from Google/Facebook/Twitter) will sell them to you on a performance basis. Most advertising networks and publishers, if they sell a CPC deal, will want the flexibility to control targeting on their end to drive the most efficient clicks possible. Outside constraints de-optimize their internal arbitrage process, limiting the profitability of an advertising deal for them.

To the extent that you can buy targeting mechanisms that you believe are effective for you on a performance basis, go for it! But rarely will these mechanisms be available.

Generally, these types of targeting mechanisms are sold to agencies that are buying specific kinds of people on a per-impression basis because their research has led them to believe that this will be more effective than other types of targeting. Given this, let's take a moment and talk about how agencies think about buying inventory.

How Agencies Buy

The starting point for advertising and marketing at an agency is a deep understanding of the product and the customer. Understanding what motivates the customer is the essence of marketing and it typically involves a non-trivial amount of research to understand the customers or types of customers that a product interacts with.

The first step is to build a user persona. That persona is a collection of demographic, psychographic and sociological traits that "define" the target customer. It may be necessary to build multiple user personas if there is more than one target customer type. A target customer might be "A 20 to 30 year old single male with $50k to $75k in annual income and a love of first person shooter video games". I just defined a simple user persona for a video game, or an action movie, or something like that.

An advertising agency does an analysis of a client's customer base and concludes that the perfect target customer, the description of a customer most likely to be inclined to buy, fits a certain demographic profile and has a specific set of interests. Generally speaking, they then develop a creative concept: A message they want to take to these people that will cause them to buy their product. Once the creative concept is crafted and ready, they may prepare to buy some media.

An RFP (request for proposal) is where media buyers reach out to media owners to identify how those media owners can help them engage their target audience. Then they receive from various media owners information about the demographic profile of people that consume that media. Procter & Gamble issues an RFP seeking to reach stay-at-home moms between the ages of 25-44. NBC responds with a proposal containing detailed demographic profiles of the audience that consumes their soap operas, information about the number of people that watch that soap opera, and pricing to buy ad space on their soap opera. Yahoo responds to the same RFP with information about women that read their "Entertainment" section and CPM pricing to buy ad impressions in that section of the web site.

From this, media planners are asked to assemble a puzzle where none of the pieces have edges. "'Friends' has the appropriate demographic, but do the people that watch it like to quilt?" "If 1% of the nation fits the profile of my target customer, and 2% of a TV programs audience is my target customer, should I buy inventory on the TV program?" It has an index of 200 - that is, the target market is twice as likely to be consuming this media than the average. Many media planners simply look at the highest indexes for making a decision. A 200 index is significant and material. I would argue that this demonstrates the challenge with index-based purchasing. Even high indexing sites can generate significant waste.

Further, media planning has become much more difficult in the online world. Twenty years ago there were only a few TV stations and newspapers to advertise with. Now there are millions of niche web sites. At the same time, media buying has become more complex. Customers want complex targeting, rich creatives and cross-campaign frequency caps. And all of this is happening in a world where there is more accountability and measurability than ever before.

When considering all of the many different ways to target an advertisement online, they can be segmented into two schools: Inventory targeted campaigns and user targeted campaigns.[15]

Inventory targeted campaigns use the type of inventory to determine the ad that should be shown. Content targeting, where ads are shown adjacent to relevant inventory, is the primary example of this. Ads for Nike shoes next to articles about baseball. Ads about skirts in women's magazines.

However the proliferation of digital targeting has tended to focus on the second school of targeting: User targeting. In television, radio, or print, it is not both possible and economical to craft a message intended for a specific user regardless of where they are. By dropping a cookie on someone, we can record their interests as cookies are updated and deployed then message them with relevant ads regardless of the site they are on.

Content

Content is where digital targeting starts and most other kinds of targeting – radio, television, newspaper – end.

---

15. Awesome and not awesome, red vs. blue, ninjas vs. pirates.

Most of television and newspaper advertising is, "I want to be in the sports section", or "I want to buy 30 seconds on American Idol". The advertiser has identified some segment of the population that they think their product will appeal to and they have determined in some way that this particular content is aligned with that audience.

Furthermore, there tends to be some alignment of "brand strength" that occurs during this kind of content matching – Gatorade runs on ESPN rather than late night infomercials because they imagine that aligning their brand with the prestige of the ESPN brand will cause some of the prestige of ESPN to rub off on the Gatorade brand. When you think of Gatorade, you will think of ESPN and vice versa.

This premium content alignment comes with a proportional increase in cost[16]. That is why the "worst" commercials are on in the middle of the night: Inexpensive inventory attracts less valuable brands. Premium brands look for premium quality content to associate with. These late night commercials tend to be hard core direct response advertisers. They know down to the penny exactly how much revenue they will generate for that ad placement and are arbitraging the ad placements to generate income. Conversely, premium brands find secondary benefits to the association with premium inventory beyond the direct revenue generated, justifying the higher cost of buying an ad spot on "American Idol".

The same thing happens online.

Thus content targeting is fundamental to nearly every kind of advertising and is the most common form of advertising seen. It is the first thing a media planner at an agency thinks about. This is not without good reason. Strong contextual targeting is very ef-

---

16. Sometimes disproportional!

fective. Studies have shown over time that strong alignment between an ad and the surrounding content can result in a more favorable attitude toward the ad, a more favorable attitude toward the product, higher intention to click on the ad and higher purchase inclinations[1].

In the context of digital advertising, content targeting can mean many things. It could mean the kind of site, like ESPN, or it could even mean the content of a page. Many travel advertisers in the digital era want more than simply targeting the travel section of a news site. They want to target pages that talk about trips to Asia with Asia-specific ads.

The inverse concept is negative content targeting. For example, Expedia will say that they do not want to appear on any news page talking about air disasters. Nobody buys a plane ticket on a page where they are reading about a plane crash. This is a great example because airlines love to buy news content talking about air travel, but not that kind of air travel news.

Agencies also frequently ask ad networks for assurances around the quality of the sites that the ad network will expose them to when running the campaign. While agencies understand the power of the optimization algorithm (or perhaps just claim to), they still want to ensure that they don't appear on certain kinds of low quality inventory such as adult content.

Many times, advertisers will have a white list or black list of inventory. A white list being a list of the only sites that they will allow their ads to run on, constraining ad delivery to that list; whereas a black list would be a list of sites that they will not run on, allowing ad delivery on any other inventory.

Google AdSense has even gone so far as to offer a targeting mechanism that restricts your campaign to running on the 1000 largest web sites on the Internet. When they announced that feature in 2010, they described it as a brand safety mechanism.

This is very common among ad networks. They typically sell "brand safe" inventory by restricting delivery to sites like the comScore top 100, top 500, or top 1000[17]. (ComScore is a measurement company that identifies the sites with the most page views and consumers, so the comScore top 100 are the 100 biggest sites in the world.) It is implied that the largest web sites in the world are generating inventory ideally suited for large brands to advertise on. Unfortunately, the amount of page views a web site generates has absolutely nothing to do with the relative brand safety or value of brand association that a web site has. Yet ad networks are incredibly incentivized to offer this kind of delivery. For most ad networks, most of their ad inventory came from these sites anyways. After all, these sites account for the majority of impressions on the Internet.

For our campaigns, we will want to discuss black listing things like casual gaming inventory, which tend to have high click through rates and terrible back-end performance because ads are placed in a way that tends to generate large amounts of accidental clicks. Everyone has had the experience of clicking an ad in a casual game when you were trying to do something in the game, then immediately hitting the back button to go back to the game.

---

17. comScore is the Nielsen of the Internet, providing a broad array of rating and analytic data about site traffic.

Demographics

Targeting demographically is about targeting users based on facts about that user. Targeting users based on their age, gender, ethnicity, income, and whether they are single or married are all examples of demographic targeting. Demographics are not opinions and they are things that may change over time, but they are immutable truth at the time: Pet owners, number of children, etc. You are never married and single at the same time. You are never two different ages simultaneously.

Demographics are something that are easy to capture and easy for marketers to understand. Ferrari knows that while young males love their ads, their products are typically purchased by people from 35 to 55 years in age, 98 percent are male and most have household incomes in excess of one million dollars per year. Marketers who understand their target demographic can match their demographic to the message and the targeting mechanisms they use to create effective advertising.

Content has demographic characteristics, so marketers can match these demographics. For example, ESPN.com users are 94% male, are predominantly between 18 and 34 years old and are generally both college-educated and employed full-time. On average, they make $72,000 per year. Forty-seven percent are single. This is a treasure trove of facts for an advertiser to make a decision about whether advertising on ESPN is an appropriate decision. Further, third party research organizations such as Nielsen or comScore could provide ESPN or an ad agency with a panel-based projection about the number of millionaires that consume ESPN content.

Psychographics

Psychographics are the next step in a marketers analysis of consumers. There are many single men, but which ones are the right ones to sell Gatorade to? While demographics tell you definitive facts about a person, psychographics are about defining their attitudes, intents, and opinions. Psychographics are the "squishy stuff" in a marketers arsenal because they are abstract and mutable.

Psychographics are especially important in online advertising as subcultures are more important than ever. One of the magic tools the Internet has brought us is that there are millions of places to go. Unlike television with a few hundred cable channels, now there is a place for every interest to enjoy their special subject. Finding people engaged around those special subjects that are meaningful to an advertiser and a brand is some of the most critical marketing activities that can be undertaken.

The challenge of psychographics is that they are much more difficult to surmise than demographics. Different people have different criteria for what qualifies someone as "interested in shoes", unlike demographics (where there is no disagreement about whether a twenty year-old is in the "Age 18-24" demographic). Frequently, the conclusion is fluid and is a combination of data and context. For example, a visit to a specialized site typically speaks more to an interest than a visit to a Yahoo page that is more targeted to the general public's interest.

Regardless, if one were selling athletic shoes, one might learn that people that buy athletic shoes tend to watch NFL football on Sundays, listen to Top 40 music and buy new shoes every six months. Based on this, marketers can tie together these behavioral elements to determine the best way to reach their target market in a much more specific manner than demographic-based targeting.

Over time, marketers can build a deep understanding of their target market as they become increasingly efficient at driving sales. They could understand specific teams, bands and other interests that are most closely tied to their target market and even start to segment the different trends between heavy buyers versus light buyers, and what makes someone move from the latter group to the former. While more complex to first understand, psychographics offers great value to a marketers advertising capability.

Index-based Targeting vs User Targeting

Let's digress for a moment and discuss index-based targeting. You may recall a comment I made earlier:

"If 1% of the nation fits the profile of my target customer, and 2% of a TV programs audience is my target customer, should I buy inventory on the TV program?"

This is a very common challenge in non-user based targeting. Because we are not targeting individual users but rather places they are likely to be, we inevitably reach people we do not intend to. The obvious question is what percentage of our spend is "wasted" on inappropriate audiences.

One way to consider this is to think about "the average". If we were trying to reach an audience that represents 0.01% of the US population (maybe left-handed PhD students?). That means that any content whose readership consists of 0.02% of that audience is generally far more likely to be reaching that audience than most other content. (0.02%/0.01% = 200, the "index" of that content for reaching that audience. That means it reaches two times as many of the target audience than the average content.)

A 200 index is typically considered very high. Unfortunately for marketers, it is fairly difficult to construct a model distribution curve that tells you what the index is for content for an audience. Further, given the sheer amount of content that exists in the world, the amount of content that exists that is one to three standard deviations outside the norm for an audience is still basically an unlimited amount.

Unfortunately, with small target audiences, even high indexing properties generate large amounts of waste. In our example, 99.8% of impressions are wasted. If one considers how to effectively price that inventory, while paying a premium to reach that audience twice as effectively as usual sounds reasonable, the amount of waste may prevent buyers from achieving their ROI in a meaningful way.

Due to the dispersion of TV audiences, most media buyers seem conditioned to find indices of over 115 demonstrative of a compelling ability to reach a given audience. In a typical RFP, it is not uncommon to be asked how your audience (as a publisher) indexes for a given target, but it is not common at all to be asked what percentage of your audience the target audience comprises. Hence situations where the target audience comprises a small but high indexing proportion of the audience can happen frequently.

Behavioral Targeting

User Targeting

Let's start by defining behaviorally targeted advertising: matching targeted ads to people based on previously gathered data rather than current page context. The hypothesis is that a broad set of historical data points allows the advertiser to better understand a person and appropriately target relevant messages to them. An advertisement can be effective if it is relevant to a specific person, regardless if that ad isn't matched to the content of the current page. This is particularly common in social networks, where it may be difficult to discern the context of a page such as a newsfeed. As I always tell people, if the only ads I ever received were for movies and video games, I would tell people that Internet advertising is totally awesome.[18]

Unlike other forms of media, the ability to maintain state and identify a user across successive requests on one site or across a network of sites allows the publisher to associate information they collected on that user in the past to their current session and factor that into a decisioning process like what kind of ad to serve to that user when they navigate through a given website. For instance, large portals that offer email services usually require data such as gender and age, and might ask for many more characteristics when users opt in to use the service. After the publisher accrues this data, they can aggregate all the accounts which they know are

---

18. I confess, I might tell people that anyway.

men, for example, and target media to those accounts, no matter where they are in their network.

Let's be clear about the implications of this: the Internet allows a marketer/publisher/site to take information from one portion of its site or a different site entirely and use it to transform content or advertising on other sites in a one-to-one fashion. Introducing this to the advertising community was the equivalent of telling them, "We can take your commercial spot on American Idol, recognize which of those viewers watched the new Britney Spears video on MTV, recognize which of those viewers saw the new Pepsi commercial, and then display to only those people a special ad completely customized to them."

This completely blew advertiser's minds.

Behavioral targeting, as it came to be called, or interest-based targeting (when people worried that behavioral targeting sounded too creepy) rapidly grew to play a key role in the industry. Every publisher suddenly realized that besides their content, they had data. And this data had value.

Of course, not very many publishers have the luxury of these proprietary data assets at any kind of scale, or if they do, aren't in the advertising business. So they, like many other marketers, rely on data aggregators and data brokers to provide the information.

Data aggregators and data brokers (called Data Management Platforms or DMPs) are technology companies that collect and aggregate anonymous user information like demographic qualities from many publishers and then sell it to marketers and other publishers that can use it. These publishers can be both content sites and service-based sites – a store where a consumer registers to buy something, dating sites where a consumer creates a profile, or social media sites where consumers disclose personal data are all rich markets for data mining beyond mere content consumption.

There are millions of potential collection points, many of which may be too small to build a dedicated business for a publisher on her own, but which are happy to collect an easy payment from the data broker for providing anonymized access to their data. Data companies gain access to this data by placing a cookie on the user when they are on these sites through a small piece of code that forces the user's browser to call the data company as they navigate on the publisher's site. With that cookie in place, the data company can deploy that data to customers via various data on their customer's websites, which provides the demographic data to ad serving technologies.

It may sound complex, but it's actually quite simple, and there are very large companies that provide demographic, interest, and other data as a valuable service to the online marketing industry, which allow marketers and publishers alike to better understand users, tailor relevant messages, and drive better and more efficient results through the ecosystem.

People will offer you all kinds of behavioral targeting to reach your audience, but you will find that it takes a truly remarkable behavior to generate high performance.

Vectors

If we want to really simplify behavioral targeting, a behavior can be distilled to three attributes:

- The event: Did this consumer visit Kelley Blue Book or visit Yahoo! Autos. A visitor to one or the other could perform differently. The places a consumer goes are prima facie pretty important!

- Recency: Was it a week ago or a month ago. Was it an hour ago? True story: Retargeting cookies you dropped in the last hour perform a zillion times better than anything else you are doing. If you are an advertiser, this is critical path stuff: Are you watching those? Are you segmenting them out and treating them differently?
- Frequency: Did they visit twice? Three times? That performs differently.

If someone visited AOL Finance twice in the last hour, that is different than three times in the last week. And both of those are different than someone who is visiting AOL Finance right now. And different than someone who has visited both AOL Finance and Motley Fool. How different? Hard to say. Depends what you are selling, but you can find out through testing and value your audience appropriately.

Publishers don't typically sell this way. It makes it hard. Suddenly the advertiser only wants to buy purple cows and that doesn't scale well. Painting in extremely broad strokes here, there are a couple of kinds of behavioral bucketing strategies that are commonly used. The simplest would be to simply describe the above behavioral attributes: "Our auto intender population is made up of people that visited AOL Autos at least 3 times in the last 60 days." This bucketing approach is nice in that it is quite transparent to an advertiser what constitutes a population member, however the population size is fixed, which can limit deliverability for a campaign. We only have X number of people with those attributes.

Typically, the way a vendor might work around this is tracking populations with varying recency and frequency. So if someone wanted to spend a bigger budget than could be delivered at 3/60 (three visits in 60 days), we have a 2/60 or a 3/90 that we could offer to advertisers and that becomes our auto intender population for this RFP. Another way to flex the population is by mixing behaviors. We might acquire auto intender data from 10 different publishers. By squishing this together, it is possible to generate larger populations – "3 visits to any of these 20 sites in the last 60 days", but it makes regressing performance more challenging, particularly because the data points around frequency, recency, and the sites used to generate the data are typically not shared with the advertiser. But then, advertisers aren't asking for it.

In an effort to recognize the performance variability in different inventory, as well as recency and frequency, many behavioral targeting sellers have transitioned to a vector approach. To illustrate from an anonymous vendor deck (and frankly, an awesome example of modern BT):

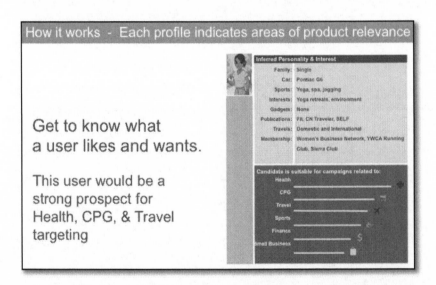

So as people surf the behavioral data providers data sources, their scores against a variety of behavioral targets are incremented and decremented based on how well the behavior provider thinks they will perform against an offer or reflect a given audience. This is nice in that it allows you to easily keep track of many variables. Rather than tracking recency and frequency and sites visited by user, you track a single number and then you have things that modify the number all the time. Data storage is much less complicated for the data provider. The downside is that you are forced to trust the publisher to accurately score users – A "strong performer" in theory could have become a strong performer in a number of ways and the advertiser can never unwind it to see if there are attributes other than "vector score of X" that correlate with performance.

Vectors are great for data exchanges because you can easily vary the vector score you are targeting to deliver appropriate campaign volume. If you have a campaign where you are trying to reach a small audience, you might target a vector score of 80 or greater (assuming a 0 to 100 scale). If you have a large budget and the same audience, you can simply target people that scored greater than 60, or 50, or 30. Whatever you need to create a population large enough to target. If you only have a few people with a vector score of 1000, you can dial it down to 600 and have a 10x bigger population. Even in the above example, it is impossible to tell when they stop being a great target because it is all relative.

Vectors today are used to gauge all kinds of things, even things like gender – "This person visits sports sites every day, ipso facto, they are male." Increment the vector! Essentially, this is a probabilistic model where it is implied that the odds that this person is a male are higher than other people.

Unfortunately, all of this ease of use is hamstrung by the fact that vectors obfuscate, even for the person generating the data, how someone became what they are. In an effort to create a compact data structure that can return real time bids in milliseconds, we have decided to limit ourselves to looking at the forest instead of trees. This is why most big data companies output models from fully-featured data sets they use for analysis.

Having a data model of historical transactions provides significantly more mechanisms to optimize and account for in advertising. With many levers, it takes significantly larger sample sizes to deeply understand performance characteristics of advertisers, but the understanding informs a more accurate truth.

The future will involve a much more rigorous analysis of performance attributes of users. The challenge that presents itself to the industry is that advertisers typically don't value this big data analysis: They pay agencies a percentage of spend to buy media. If an agency spends tens of thousands of dollars determining that hundreds of thousands of dollars do not need to be spent to reach the audience most likely to convert, how are parties compensated for that work? If publishers suddenly find that ninety percent of their audience is not valued by advertisers, can they price the last ten percent in such a way as to return the value needed for publishing to be successful? Given the history of pricing models as they have transferred from print and TV to digital, it has been difficult to price individual users at the premium they probably deserve given the value of the targeting provided.

Further, in the digital space there is extremely limited budget for creative development. Absent a micro-site such as Subservient Chicken, Burger King's immensely successful viral ad campaign, it is difficult for an agency to justify large expenditures on making great banners. Yet the information available now implies that there may be an opportunity to build extremely customized experiences for very small audiences. Historical pricing models for media buying make it difficult for agencies to invest in this fashion.

Despite this, there can be no questioning that advertisers value intimacy with users. A deep understanding of consumers and a deep understanding of the characteristics of consumers that create appropriate behaviors is an immense value to advertisers and highly sought after.

The Technology Nitty-Gritty

Cookies & Web Beacons

Let's dive a bit further into the technology nitty-gritty of how this works. Cookies and web beacons are something we have already spent a lot of time driving through. In the context of web behaviors, a pixel could be placed on a page with the intention of capturing a behavior. This pixel is frequently associated with a specific behavior that is captured from the context of the page. If a page is about football, the pixel firing could indicate to the server that this user, with a cookie ID of X, has expressed an interest in football. This is then tracked and used for future targeting purposes. The pixel could be dynamically populated as well. If registration data were being captured, maybe the pixel has an age or gender parameter that the site populates with values on the fly, using registration information from the user login to pass that demographic data to the third party behavior server. It is not uncommon today for many websites to have literally dozens of pixels on a page passing data to a range of services and third parties.

One common example of behavioral targeting is retargeting. This extremely widespread Internet e-commerce advertising technique involves showing ads to people marketing products that they have viewed at some point. Amazon loves to use this technique, showing consumers ads for products that they put in their shopping cart, but never purchased. This technique demonstrates the power of pixels. A pixel is set on the product page and when the consumer visits, that page dynamically populates a value that indicates what product the consumer was looking at. This allows the advertiser to know what products the consumer is interested in by studying their cookie when they are found again later. To add further sophistication to the technique, a pixel could be placed on a checkout page (or the "Thank You" page, as it is known) to indicate that the consumer has successfully purchased the product. This pixel could over-write the previously assigned cookie value with a new value to indicate that the consumer should no longer be targeted with that particular message because the consumer has successfully purchased the product.

Another example of more complex pixels is the Google AdSense ad unit. The AdSense ad unit, the first time it is called on a page becomes aware that it has never been called and sends a message to the Google Spider to crawl the page and determine the context of that page (much in the same way that Google Spider generates relevant search results for a page). This allows AdSense to, upon later requests, identify the nature of the content on the page and return a relevant advertisement. In this respect, the ad unit itself dynamically behaves much like a pixel.

Behavior Servers

Post-pixel, all of this information about consumers is then stored either directly in the cookie or in a behavior server or profile server. Generally speaking, a profile server allows the advertiser to store a user ID in the cookie, then store all of the consumer's behavioral attributes in a database. When an ad request occurs and a cookie is shared, behavioral attributes of a consumer may be looked up and discovered based on the ID, then factored into the ad serving process.

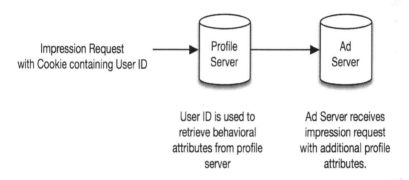

Due to the tremendous amount of data that may be processed as ads are served and pixels are fired, some populations may be built retrospectively in a batch process. For example, if an advertiser wanted to reach a consumer that expressed a very complex behavior, it might make more sense from an engineering perspective to review the behaviors expressed by consumers ever few hours or every day to determine if that consumer is "in the population" rather than evaluating consumer fit as each new individual behavior is expressed and logged.

Conversely, much of cookie-targeted ad serving is now real-time. For example, a key aspect of almost every digital ad serving business is frequency capping advertisements.

Frequency Caps

A frequency cap is a tool used to limit the number of times an advertisement is delivered to a user within a specific time frame. Caps can limit the number of times an ad is shown per user, campaign, hour, browser session and more.

When the user views an ad, the advertiser uses a cookie to indicate that they have been exposed to the ad. The next time the consumer is seen, the cookie is received and then the fact that the consumer has already seen the ad is factored into the ad serving decision. If the cap has not been reached, this can be factored in as well. Once the cap has been reached, the server recognizes this fact and serves a different ad to that user.

Frequency capping also allows publishers to control how often users see an ad that may interfere with the consumer's experience or the site's content, such as a pop-up or full-screen interstitial advertisement.

Frequency capping is important because it can have a significant impact on the performance of a campaign. In the abstract, the concept is straightforward: If a consumer sees the same ad one hundred times, the odds that many of these exposures are wasted are high. Most advertisers, given a choice between reach and frequency, choose reach. Consider this: Would you rather show two people an ad fifty times or fifty people an ad twice? Reach wins!

Our logic is born out by research as well. Studies have shown that as ad exposure increases, it soon crosses an inflection point where performance is poor[2]. The "perfect" frequency for an ad probably varies from audience to audience and creative message to creative message, but experience has shown that it is rarely more than five.

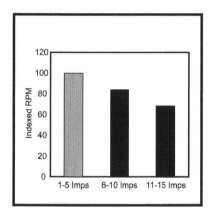

So there you have it. Once you have seen an ad five times, the odds that you will turn into a customer, if you haven't already, has declined sharply.

Types of Behaviors

Direct Response targeting is just like much of the direct mail that you receive in your mail box. It is designed to get you to do something at that very moment. It is designed to engender an immediate and direct response from the target. Branding is at the other end of the spectrum. It can be thought of as an attempt to increase goodwill. For example, when you see a Coke commercial on TV or most car commercials, those advertisers generally do not expect you to leap off your couch and run to the store (although they would love it if you did!). They want to make you think positively about the brand. When you go to the store next time, they want you to feel a positive connection to Coca-Cola. When you see the Coke sign or when you think about how you are thirsty, you will think of how Mean Joe Greene quenches his thirst the old-school way with a Coca-Cola and then you will want to quench your thirst similarly.

Some people (Me? Although never in a bad way.) refer to branding as "the squishy stuff". It is typically harder to tie to revenue. Direct Response is expected to be directly connected to revenue. For every dollar of direct response ("DR") money you spend, you should see more than a dollar in revenue. Otherwise it is simply not working because the definition of direct response is this.

While every kind of advertising technique can be used for both purposes, generally speaking a targeting mechanism will be on a spectrum of effectiveness, where some techniques are more effective in generating direct responses than others. Consider contextual targeting for a moment. Advertisers are certainly interested in contextual targeting for both direct response and brand associations and for a given brand, there are advertising opportunities that will vary in effectiveness for each of these. Under Armour presents a fine example. Under Armour frequently markets its products on NFL broadcasts or ESPN. This is primarily branding. Few people see this and think "I need Under Armour!" UA simply wants you to think about how much Calvin Johnson loves UA when he is exercising and the next time you think about exercise, hopefully you will consider buying UA. Conversely, Under Armour also markets on sites for things like exercise products. On these sites, consumers are actively looking for products to purchase to help them exercise. This kind of contextual advertising is designed to engender a more direct response. They want you to click and buy.

There are many kinds of behavioral targeting and each of these also has implications for branding and direct response advertising.

Search

We have said it before and we will say it again: Google has built a fantastic business. Search advertising is a powerful interest-based advertising technique that is near legendary in its effectiveness as a direct response technique. We have already talked extensively about search, so I will not belabor the point.

Put simply, when someone googles a product or service, it is likely that they are in-market to buy said thing. If they google "Big Screen TV" and are subsequently shown ads for big screen TVs, the rate at which they click those ads and then buy those products is unheard of in the history of advertising.

Search is today some of the most effective advertising in the world. Advertisers are able to identify pure consumer intent and directly speak to it.

Consider this Google search for "big screen TV":

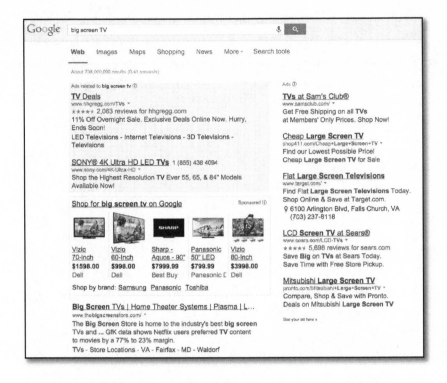

This search result page shows how targeted Google can be. The only search result on screen that is not an advertisement is the very last line on the page. There are fifteen ad results on this page and every one is highly relevant to the query. The odds that the consumer finds these ads relevant and engaging to their consumer experience is very high.

Post-Search

Post-Search targeting is a related and intriguing targeting technique. While Google has a virtual monopoly on access to search data, there is data leakage using the HTTP referer[19]. The HTTP referer is an aspect of the HTTP protocol that we have not discussed, so let's discuss it briefly. On every HTTP request, most modern browsers pass a referer. This is extremely useful in analytics as it indicates where a person came from. Allow me to illustrate:

```
GET /blog/ HTTP/1.1
User-Agent: Mozilla/5.0
Referer: http://www.cogmap.com/
```

This is a straightforward GET request with a referrer. This request illustrates a request for the "/blog/" page on this site and the request was referred from a page with the URL "http://www.cogmap.com/". That is to say, the page the consumer was on prior to this request was that page. This is how sites identify that, for example, they were on the front page of TechCrunch or CNN or other popular news sites. They are seeing tons of traffic with those sites as the referrer and this tells you that they are driving traffic to you.

Analytics firms also frequently use this to reveal keywords that are driving traffic to a site. This is because Google frequently passes keywords in their referer. Consider this example referer and its implications:

```
Referer:
http://www.google.com/search/q=JP+Morgan+org+cha
rt
```

19. "Referrer" was mis-spelled in the original RFC adding the referrer concept to the HTTP specification. It was not noticed until it was too late. Hence today "referer" is used. I can't make this stuff up.

Here, the consumers browser has indicated that they came from a search engine result page (SERP) where the query was "JP Morgan org chart". Of course, it took only moments for savvy advertisers to realize that this was not just an analytic boon. Suddenly, I know that you came to Cogmap because you were searching for "JP Morgan org chart"! Not only can I use this analytically to improve my site in the future, I can begin crafting a custom experience for you. Further, I can cookie you and when I see you in the future, I can know that you first came here looking for "JP Morgan org chart" and customize future data toward you. Finally, I can syndicate this knowledge to third parties or to my own network and use this on other sites for targeting as an interest: Maybe this indicates that you have some interest in financial services industries. But more valuably, this is an example of remarkably specific data. While other behavioral targeting techniques might lump information such as this into general "business interest" buckets, post-search techniques rely on technology similar to search to maximize the value of this extremely pointed search that the user had been conducting previously.

This can make post-search a valuable direct response technique, however the challenge of post-search is that consideration must be taken concerning how the nature of a consumer's interest changes as real-time intent transforms into historical intentions. For example, someone searching for "big screen TV" on Google now might not be an interesting target for "big screen TV" post-search ads in thirty days. Of course, someone searching for "NYT Best Sellers" might have a reasonable (albeit probably lower) likelihood of conversion if shown an ad for NYT Best Sellers at some point in the future.

Hence effective post-search targeting requires consideration of how to leverage the highly specific data provided by search referral, yet a thoughtfulness regarding how to engage searchers in a way that recognizes the ephemeral nature of intention over time.

Unfortunately for advertisers, Google has taken steps of late to limit this data leakage and begun obfuscating the search terms, making scale in post-search targeting an on-going challenge.

Contextual Interest

Contextual interest behaviors are what most people in the industry think of when they consider behavioral targeting and is addressed by many of the examples we have used up until now. Things like "visiting a finance site" or "visiting a sports site" are examples of these behaviors. This represents the most profligate behavior expressed on the Internet today because it is being expressed every time someone visits a page. Even visiting google.com expresses "an interest in searching for things". (Albeit a not very useful or interesting behavior due to its ubiquity.)

Unfortunately, this is probably one of the least interesting kinds of behavioral targeting. If someone "visited a finance site" recently, that is probably less valuable and less performant for an advertiser than someone visiting a finance site right now. Now, there is probably a combination of frequency and recency where a consumer might become more valuable – maybe an advertiser would find someone that had visited a finance site every day for the last week more valuable than someone who is visiting right now. But that is a fairly small population. Probably, given these facts, the easiest way to reach that person would be to simply advertise on the finance site. But you get the idea. There are definitely behaviors that are highly sought after: Auto manufacturers covet people recently shopping on automotive sites.

It is also important to draw a line between contextual and "content" targeting. The industry convention is to refer to contextual targeting as being based on the actual content of the page. For example, if one were reading the travel section of the New York Times and you were reading an article about Las Vegas flights, then the contextual targeting on the page would be specifically about Las Vegas. Industry convention dictates that content targeting usually involves rolling up a page into some sort of genre. In fact, the IAB (Internet Advertising Bureau, the standards body of Internet Advertising) has defined more than 100 "content categories" that represent a standard ontology of Internet content.[3] This content categorization schema is used in many different places for advertising.

Retargeting

Retargeting (or remarketing as it is infrequently called) is one of the most compelling and popular forms of advertising online. Retargeting involves identifying consumer interest in goods or services, placing a cookie on them indicating this attribute, and then targeting them with messages concerning that good or service later. We have already introduced the concept of retargeting, so let me add a few important notes.

As we previously discussed, an advertiser places a web beacon on his site to cookie consumers as they visit his pages. This cookie is then used to "re-target" that consumer when they are seen later on other sites. There are many innovative ways that retargeting can be used or enhanced to be more effective. A special cookie could be set for people that have items in their shopping cart but have not checked out. This is a great conversion opportunity. Continuing that thread, a special cookie could be set for people after they check out. This might ensure that they do not receive retargeting messages about products they have already bought, but instead receive special messages if they don't come back and buy something new after a pre-determined length of time.

I cannot underscore enough how effective retargeting historically is for advertisers. While search is compelling (searching for "big screen TV" indicates an interest in buying a big screen TV), retargeting can be equally compelling or more compelling in the right situation. If they searched for "big screen TV", that is great, but if they came to your site and looked at a specific big screen TV on your site, that is even better. It indicates not just an interest in buying a big screen TV, but an interest in your brand and your site and an interest in buying that TV from you.

Some studies have shown CTR increases of as much as 3x compared to traditional digital advertising.[4] Performance on the backend is similar. Think about it: If I am sending a custom marketing message to people with abandoned shopping carts on my site, the odds of convincing them to purchase versus sending a general message to general internet users trying to entice them to come to my site and purchase are not comparable. The former is like money in the bank.

Most advertisers already know this. Retargeting is their favorite thing to buy after search. But retargeting also makes advertisers sad because there isn't very much of it. Retargeting is naturally constrained by the need to create targetable consumers to retarget. In our prior example of targeting abandoned shopping carts, that implies that the maximum opportunity that campaign has is the number of consumers that have an abandoned shopping cart. That is not a lot of people.

The result of this today is that most advertisers buy all of the retargeting they can. And it is still a small part of their budget. Also, from a targeting perspective, they typically do not get too fancy with the targeting. Any person that has visited their site is a more likely prospect than someone who has never visited their site. So it makes sense to show lots of ads to those people. And historically, the value and return on that investment has continued to be strong so advertisers continue to do it.

Retargeting and Creepiness

One thing that needs to be addressed in the context of retargeting is just how creepy it is. At this point, I think everyone has had the experience of being retargeted. It's that awareness of seeing and ad for a predict you were just viewing mere moments ago. That's retargeting. People do it because it is effective, but it's a shame it is starting to feel like an invasion of privacy. I want to digress for a moment with a story of how retargeting got started and the slippery slope to creepiness.

John Ferber, one of the founders of Advertising.com, invented retargeting. He had a bolt of lightning in his brain one day that made him see how the technology that was being used for conversion pixels could be applied to deliver ads to people after they had visited a website and he named this "Advertiser LeadBack". (Advertiser LeadBack is a designated trademark of Advertising.com, a wholly owned subsidiary of AOL) Advertiser LeadBack was a phenomenally successful product. So successful, in fact, that advertisers would ask other companies for "LeadBack". Ad.com felt like they were the Coca-Cola of the trade, the brand identity of their retargeting solution was so popular and well-known.

One battle continually fought at Advertising.com was the battle to cut down the number of retargeting partners an agency worked with. Essentially, the thesis was this:

- Advertisers wanted to spend more on retargeting because it performed so well, but they still frequency capped campaigns because everyone agreed that high frequency was not improving performance.
- Ad.com had the biggest network from a reach perspective.
- Most of the other networks were buying the same inventory to get reach, just different frequencies.
- Ipso facto, buying a campaign on another ad network was typically simply increasing the frequency to a user rather than reaching new users.
- Buying retargeting campaigns from other companies was wasteful.

As it turns out, every time Ad.com won that battle and deprived competitors of retargeting budgets, I now think there was another effect: It decreased creepiness online.

I attribute four things to the rise in the creepiness factor:

Small advertisers having access to retargeting technology. At Advertising.com, there were huge minimums: $25,000 in ad spend per month. Only the biggest advertisers in the world advertised with them. If you advertised with them, you were spending a significant amount of money advertising online. Only a tiny sliver of your budget was being devoted to retargeting. The result was that people saw the advertisers ads all over the place and most of them weren't retargeted. Further, people had become accustomed to the idea that big advertisers ads would appear in random places as part of a network buy. So if you went to a big web site and then saw an ad for that website somewhere, you could write it off to big marketing campaigns. Not too creepy. With the influx of small advertisers, now people see ads all the time that they know had to be targeted to them. These small advertisers are not buying ad space on all these sites! They are only here because I am here. Creepy!

Customized creatives. It is one thing to see a Best Buy ad. Best Buy is a big brand, they spend a lot on marketing. It is another to see the TV that I was just looking at being shown to me again. The growth in sophistication of retargeting creatives powered by retargeting-centric companies like Criteo and TellApart make you aware of just how closely you are being watched. Despite this, a recent study published by the American Marketing Association indicated that as consumers demonstrate deepening interest in a product area, more targeted ads with more product information perform increasingly well.[5]

The dramatic increase in retargetable inventory. When most people bought most of their retargeting via Advertising.com, Ad.com actually worked very hard to limit the amount of frequency that we bought. This was because typically they didn't have that many ads to show any given person. The result is that you would only see a couple of ads.

To extend the Best Buy metaphor, you would go to twenty or thirty web sites and you would see a specific ad that had been retargeted to you on one or two. The campaigns were frequency capped and they simply didn't have that much inventory. A few billion impressions per day. Now, with the advent of exchanges, networks and DSPs can peek at 10 billion plus impressions every day and people are much looser with frequency caps because the ROI continues to be strong. The result is that you might see these retargeted ads on 10 or 15 of these web sites. Even the biggest advertisers probably aren't buying all the inventory directly! They must be following you.

My final point is, in some ways, simply an extension of the above: Quality of inventory is declining. I don't mean quality in an absolute sense, but in that abstract sense that advertisers tend to think of quality: Big Brands. As long tail inventory gets exposed to exchanges, it just feels less like an advertiser bought the space and more like the advertiser bought you. Best Buy inventory appearing in Yahoo Mail? But of course! Best Buy ads appearing on random blog about punk rock? Creepy.

I recognize there is no going back, but to deny the sensation of increasing encroachment on privacy is intellectually dishonest. We always discussed how it would be "best" if people felt like these ads were not following them at all. The point of these ads, from a squishy brand perspective, is that when a consumer sees these ads, they bolster the credibility of the advertiser – "Wow, that web site is big enough to be advertising on some of my favorite sites, I trust that web site more." As the focus has turned more and more to yield, much like the shady infomercials of late night television, performance has dictated the outcome far more so than an attempt to engender brand credibility.

Privacy

We talked about creepiness in retargeting, but it is high time we addressed head on some of the privacy concerns people have.

Of course, the more information that is gathered by the data brokers, the more risk of invasive privacy concerns exist for consumers. No consumer wants all of their web surfing history to be available for sale. Of course, advertiser and vendor perspectives are that much more invasive transactional data is available in offline data co-ops. Everything that a person buys with their credit card, every magazine they subscribe to, credit scores and other financial data are all readily available for purchase in a variety of direct marketing constructs.

Having said that, there seems to be a correlation between relevance and discovery of consumer characteristics and implications for privacy. As more information is discovered, value to advertisers increases, but compromise to consumers right to protect sensitive data accelerates.

An example that many people are familiar with was Aol's release of search data. In 2006, Aol released to the public a data set for research that consisted of 20 million search queries across 625,000 users. While the data was theoretically anonymized, the nature of the queries allowed many people to be identified (e.g. People google themselves a lot). This illustrates how intent data can be turned into personally identifiable information (PII), the bane of the industry. PII data allows a user to be identified. According to EU law, this requires that the user explicitly permit this. Obviously, for much of advertising, giving a user a moment where they are told that they are explicitly identified and being targeted and tracked and offering them the opportunity to opt-in to such an event is completely impractical (and frequently impossible). Also, generally, US law requires a very different kind of privacy policy for a site that allows vendors to gather PII. This kind of compliance is difficult if not impossible to ensure. Hence, gathering PII is regarded as a risky and dangerous legal event for much of online advertising.

Besides legal issues of PII, there are ethical and legal considerations related to simple behavioral targeting. Sensitive populations are a great example of areas where tracking users represents an area of potential risk. Ethnicity-based targeting, sexual orientation, and health and medical information are all things that ride a fine line of moral and ethical comfort for behavioral targeting. A classic example is that a third party, looking over someone's shoulder while they surf the Internet, might see behaviorally targeted ads for a medical condition, causing them to make certain assumptions about that person. So that person's interest in the medical condition becomes unbounded from just the time they spend on a medical site.

The Internet Advertising Bureau, the general standards-making body of internet advertising, has developed a self-regulatory approach to managing privacy concerns associated with internet advertising. This consists of seven principles that I will paraphrase:

- Education: People should be able to understand what information is gathered and how it is used for targeting.
- Transparency: People should know when ads are targeted to them based on data that has been gathered about them. Theoretically, this includes data collection, but in practice this means that web site privacy policies that are never read by consumers are just that much longer. If disclosure occurred at the moment of data collection, with dozens of pixels on virtually every page on the Internet today, it would make the Internet a dull

and tedious place. Of course, it would probably dramatically discourage online advertising.

- Consumer Control: People should be able to opt-out of
  targeting. More on this in a minute.
- Data Security: You would like to think that this information should be kept private.
- Material Changes: Consumers should be informed
  when a sites privacy policy changes. This usually manifests itself much like a voicemail exchange: The first
  line of the privacy policy reads, "The privacy policy recently changed. Please read it carefully."
- Sensitive Data: No targeting kids. Also, medical conditions, financial data, and social security numbers are a
  no-no.
- Accountability: There should be some ability to regu-
  late people.

Consumer Control is one of the more interesting aspects of the
program. The ability to opt-out is fairly consistently implemented
today by a consumer being able to "opt-out" which manifests itself
as placing a cookie on their browser which indicates that no targeting should happen. Ironically, this means that if a consumer
chooses to delete their cookies, then the opt-out has been deleted
as well.

Do Not Track (DNT) is a new approach to opt-out that involves setting an HTTP header in the browser. This would allow a
browser to be "configured" to not participate in behavioral targeting. In fact, the most recent release of Internet Explorer has Do
Not Track turned on by default for consumers. The response from
industry has been to not honor the Do Not Track standard. Business such as Facebook, Google, and Aol have not implemented
support for Do Not Track. Obviously, it is in the advertising in-

dustries best interests to track consumers as much as possible. When something like DNT is rolled out as the default to consumers, requiring consumers to opt-in to receive behaviorally targeted advertising, this puts the industry at a substantial disadvantage. Conversely, all signs point to consumers generally preferring to be opted out of behaviorally targeted advertising by default.

While many standards bodies are working on resolving this tension, they are all at a near impasse as the tension between consumers and advertisers appears irreconcilable.

Roster Targeting

Roster targeting, or "registration targeting" is a common online sales tool today with significant growth potential. As large sites gather registration data on consumers, the ability to match that registration data to other online or offline data sources is extremely intriguing to advertisers.

For example, Macy's could generate a list of "valued customers" that they share with Yahoo. Yahoo could match that list of names/addresses/email/phone numbers with registration data they keep on file creating a "roster" of matching identities. These people can then be targeted with custom messages from Macy's across Yahoo's network.

Did you know that when they ask you for your zip code when you use your credit card to buy things at the store, they actually use that data on the backend to match you to other transactional data. There is only one Brent Halliburton that lives in DC. With the knowledge of where you live and your name, making a match with a broad set of data to better understand customers, sell their data to the same data co-ops, and acquire data for future ad targeting is elementary.

Sequential Messaging

Sequential messaging is a tool that intrigues advertisers, but rarely delivers in the manner anticipated. The theory is simple: If I can cookie a user when they visit content and I can cookie a user when I show them an ad for frequency capping, then I could cookie a user to indicate that I had shown them an ad, then show them a different ad based on that cookie. This would allow me to show a consumer a sequence of ads to slowly evolve a concept over time.

This sounds very powerful at face value. Also, it is something that is really only possible online (You cannot show me an ad on TV knowing that I watched American Idol yesterday, but the prospect makes advertisers drool!) Unfortunately, the economics rarely work. Even with a massive reach vehicle, typically ten consumers need to see the first ad to ensure that a single consumer is found later that has that cookie set. Following this through to its logical extreme, in a three message sequential messaging campaign, one hundred of the first ad must be shown to deliver the third message to a single consumer. That means that the spend allocation is similar: 100:1.[20]

So while sequential marketing is a compelling and enticing tool in an advertisers mind, and a potentially remarkable attention getting mechanism, it is rarely seen in practice. No advertiser wants

---

20. Well, it probably isn't that bad. A consumer that is found a first time is much more likely to be found a second time. But you get the idea.

to budget $10,000 for one ad in order to show $100 worth of the third ad.

Efficacy of Out-of-Context Messaging

A frequent question by first time behavioral targeters is "but does out of context advertising work?" This is a fair question. Out of context advertising is definitely different and this needs to be taken into account. Having said that, acceptable context while being out of context is probably, for lack of a better word, acceptable. By this I mean that there is a certain standard of content quality that probably is important to brand affiliation. For example, most advertisers do not want their ads, no matter how well behaviorally targeted, to appear next to something like pornographic content. This remains true even if this person is definitely an in-market auto shopper based on their previously observed behavior.

Having said that, generally speaking, most content, such as Facebook, is fine and performs fine. Gatorade would prefer to appear on ESPN, but appearing on Yahoo! Finance to a frequent ESPN visitor is not a big deal. One opportunity for marketers is to consider how to take advantage of different contexts by doing things like tailoring the message to different content categories. Having said that, creating a broad range of creative or a complex dynamic message have hurdles and this is rarely done.

Facebook Targeting

Facebook provides a very powerful form of interest-based targeting. Very, very few pages on the Facebook platform are contextually targeted. Instead, Facebook uses behavioral targeting across almost all of their platform, exposing registration data they have gathered from their users to create an exciting marketing opportunity.

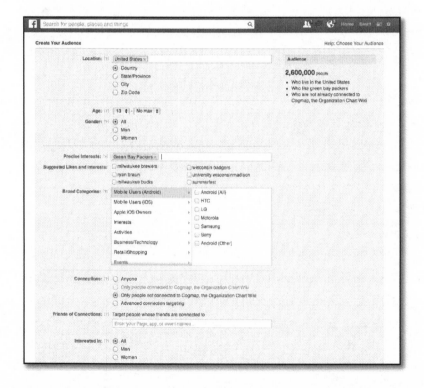

Because Facebook is awash in consumers that have actively identified their interests, Facebook makes those interests explicitly targetable in their ad targeting system. In the above example, you can see that there are 2.6 million people who have identified the

Green Bay Packers as one of their favorite things. This can be a powerful tool for precisely reaching an audience. The sheer amount of audience data, the amazing reach of the Facebook platform, and the performance-based CPC pricing of Facebook make this a valuable behavioral targeting platform for advertisers.

Facebook has grown their traffic so quickly (their site has more page views than any site in the world) that even though their advertising base has grown rapidly, there are still many pockets of inexpensive clicks available. The key to using Facebook effectively as a start-up is to run many creatives, each laser targeted to a demographic, a geography, or both. The creatives need strong images and calls to action that are regionalized or personalized in some way because the way that Facebook's algorithm works to optimize eRPM of a page, if you can get high CTRs, then you will be able to get very inexpensive clicks. If your CTRs are low, you will find that the bid price is very high.

Data Management Platforms

Clearly behavioral targeting offers a significant opportunity for advertisers and an opportunity that they are eager to take advantage of. This translates into a meaningful opportunity for publishers to the extent that they are interested in monetizing data by collecting, normalizing, segmenting and activating anonymous digital data.

Many publishers struggle with how to manage their data and their relationship with third party data monetization. Some fear that allowing third parties to access their data will cannibalize the value of their inventory. (Some publishers are correct in this regard.) However, most agree that the nature of digital advertising has bifurcated budgets and getting access to network spend, RTB markets, and third party data stream revenue is incremental revenue.

Data Management Platforms, or DMPs, are third party data mediation platforms that provide tools for publishers to easily share data and provide tools to advertisers to allow them to easily consume data. DMPs simplify data management in this way and streamline the incremental revenue generation offered by data sharing.

DMPs add value further through analytics, cross-site combinations and more complex targeting capabilities than a publisher and advertiser could create in a silo. Finally, and probably most importantly for publishers, DMPs are motivated to help sell the data at scale. Theoretically, DMPs simply have more opportunities to license the data to advertisers than the publisher might have on her own as they meet with a variety of advertisers seeking a broad array of data.

Also, DMPs are increasingly involved on the buy-side. For example, Kraft recently used a DMP[6] to correlate first party information they had from on-site activity with third party data sets to develop a more complete view of their consumers.

DMPs will be more fully featured and more pervasive over the next several years as the advertising industry continues to explore the many different ways that third party data sets can create value from the top to the bottom of the marketing funnel.

Mobile Advertising and Location

Location Targeting

Media consumption using mobile devices in 2012 constituted 12% of total media consumption in the US. It was also the only form of media consumption that was growing and its growth came at the expense of TV, radio, and print.

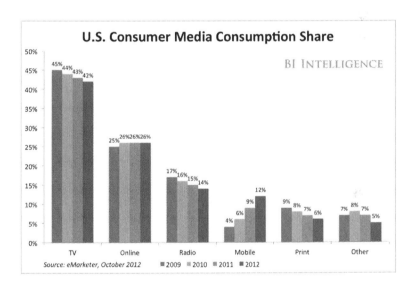

The growth of mobile is expected to continue – this is just the first inning of the ball game! We are in the midst of a fundamental change. For the first time, in 2012, sales of smartphones and tablets exceeded sales of computers. And the growth is continuing to accelerate globally. Where people have desktop computers and general share them among family members and generally replace them every four or five years, now they have smartphones that they replace every two years and every member of the family has their own device.

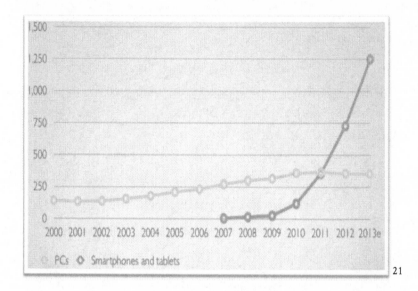

21

To take it one step further, the emergence of smartphones starting with the iPhone has fundamentally changed the way people think about technology. Previously, mobile phones were bigger than computers. The integration of smartphones into the broader technology platforms built around the Internet has dramatically changed the way people think about the market.

---

21. Enders Analysis

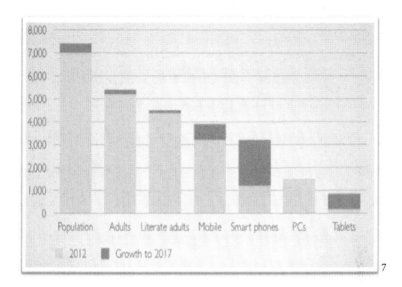

For the first time, when people are out in the world, they are suddenly carrying a uniquely personal device. Furthermore, they are using it all the time. They are now out in the world with their head down, engrossed in their personal device. To quote Sir Martin Sorrell, the CEO of WPP (the world's largest advertising agency): "Location targeting is the holy grail that we as advisers on behalf of our clients are looking for."

Location targeting and mobile targeting are inextricably linked. When advertisers think about mobile advertising, they consider it in the context of location. The cliché dream is to reach someone as they walk by the Starbucks store with a Starbucks coupon, causing them to turn into the store and spend money.

Even in the most general case, geo-targeting is important to almost every kind of advertiser. Precious few advertisements have truly national relevance. Obviously, small and medium size businesses (a huge portion of advertising dollars spent every year) typically have a regional footprint. Further, products like antifreeze have a geographic focus. People in Florida don't buy a lot of anti-freeze. And consider franchises such as Subway and McDonalds (and almost any retailer or automotive company) – much of their marketing budget consists of regional marketing dollars. Elections? Almost every dollar is spent focused on geographically key areas.

The need for location-based targeting clearly exists not just in mobile, but on the desktop. Let's talk about how the industry has addressed that problem and then talk about how it is used.

Location targeting on the desktop has historically been done by using the IP address. Every computer has an IP address. It is a string of numbers (128.0.0.1, for example) that uniquely identifies your computer on the Internet. IP addresses are a key part of what makes the Internet work. If Google wants to send the results of a search to your computer, how do they know which computer is yours? Your IP address!

Every computer referenced in a URL has an IP address and it is a routers job to store lists that guide it as it forwards a message packet around the Internet. These lists also contain DNS (domain name service) lookup tables that translate things like "www.google.com" into an IP address.

As you may know, the Internet was originally designed (by Al Gore?) to survive a military attack. With multiple routers distributed around the Internet, even if one router goes down, packets can be dynamically routed around it. So typically, in a few milliseconds, a message packet will pass through a half-dozen computers on its way to a final destination.

These computers all have some physical location and many companies such as MaxMind, NetAcuity, and Quova are attempting to plot those locations. Typically the way these companies work is that they have dozens (or in some cases, hundreds) of people working out of a call center, using special Internet protocols and also simple phones to try to identify the physical location of IP addresses. Unfortunately, they have been right as frequently as they have been wrong. A classic example that many reference was that during Aol's heyday, when millions of consumers dialed their modems to access the Internet through Aol, to IP targeters, it seemed as though more than 20% of Internet users lived in Northern Virginia (the home office of Aol). This is because they would see huge volumes of traffic from devices that were tied to the domain aol.com. Absent better information, that location was tied to Northern Virginia. This kind of problem is true of any large company that has firewalls and internal routers. Places like Apple have many, many offices and locations, however, most IP-Geo databases believe that Apple is in Cupertino, CA. Finally, many people connect to the Internet through large ISPs such as Comcast or Verizon. These connections are likely impossible to tie together as many of them use what are called "dynamic" IP addresses. That is, the IP address will be assigned to a specific machine for a brief period of time, then re-assigned to a different machine. This facilitates more efficient use of IP addresses than a "static" IP address system, but the result is that geo-location by IP address is tenuous at best.

Having said that, many advertisers have grown sufficiently comfortable with IP-based targeting to use it to target at the state level or DMA level.

Smartphones have changed the way that many advertisers think about this advertising opportunity. With each device containing a GPS system, it suddenly seems possible to build a revolutionary new advertising platform that utilizes much more precise location data.

GPS works in several ways. First, there is the traditional GPS that most of us think of when we consider GPS: Sending a signal to a satellite or series of satellites that triangulates the device location. This is effective, but time consuming. To overcome this, the industry has developed "assisted GPS", whereby cell towers use their knowledge of a GPS satellites approximate location relative to the cell tower to artificially mimic GPS. For practical purposes of ad targeting, those are indistinguishable.

Finally, there is wi-fi signal triangulation. Have you ever wondered why your iPhone tells you that location data will be more accurate if you turn on wifi? This concept, popularized by a company called Skyhook Wireless, uses the fact that most wifi networks are stationary to build a web of location-based detection. Essentially, if you are at your house, you might see your home wifi network with strong signal strength and several neighbors with slightly lower signal strength. Given data about the location of your neighbors and the signal strength (relative distance) of their networks on your device, triangulating your location is straightforward. So companies like Skyhook, Google, and Microsoft drive cars around neighborhoods building mappings of the physical location of wifi networks to facilitate effective triangulation.

Your smartphone does all of these in an effort to pinpoint your location to within tens of meters.

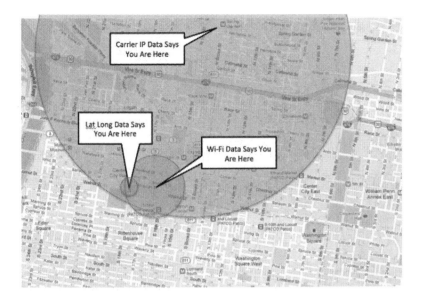

Key takeaway: While everyone wants geo-targeting, geo-targeting on the desktop is not great. Conversely, in mobile geo-targeting seems very congruent with the mechanism of engagement as people are out and about in their community. So when people think about mobile targeting, they are thinking about location-based targeting. Fortunately, the targeting works better.

Increasingly, as people recognize the importance of quality location data, they are looking for third parties that can audit this data. Unfortunately, this market is still in the very early stages. comScore offers such a product, however because they don't have direct access to the device, their product at one point was simply an IP-lookup system that used one of the freely available databases.

Geofences

Location data is very powerful. Given knowledge of a person's current location it is possible to infer demographic information, socioeconomic status and interests. However, in the big scheme of things, the most interesting thing about location data is that it reveals the location of the consumer. Knowledge of a consumer's present location reveals a set of interests that create relevant and timely targeting opportunities. In the prior example, knowing they are in front of a coffee shop makes them interesting to that coffee shop.

In the parlance of the day, this is called geo-fencing. Conceptually, a wall is drawn around a given location and if a consumer is seen inside the wall, they are targeted. This is very appealing to businesses. If you are near the store, the store wants you to stop by. Geo-fences can vary in radius. YellowPages studied the relative performance of 1.5 billion impressions served for various local businesses in their network and saw the best performance at one to two miles.

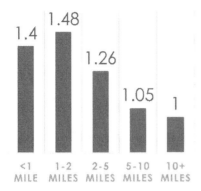

1.5 billion impression study by YP Local Mobile Display Network, 2Q2012 8

Verve performed a similar study of CTR for retailers in its network based on the distance of the consumer from the retailer and saw similar conclusions with a sweet spot that extended out five miles:

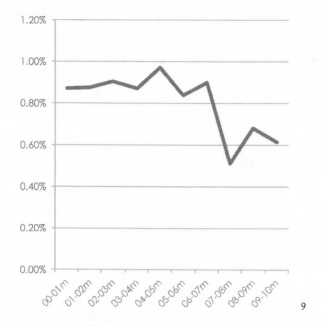

9

These studies are merely examples but they illustrate an important point: Proximity impacts performance. It is likely that this performance varies by the kind of store you have (e.g. A Home Depot can attract people from further away than a McDonalds) and population density (e.g. In Manhattan, there is a Starbucks on every block, ipso facto, advertising a specific Starbucks a mile away is unlikely to effective. Whereas in North Dakota, a mile might be thought of as incredibly close.)

Another important use of geofencing is called "geo-conquesting". In geo-conquesting, a geo-fence is drawn around competitor locations. For example, McDonald's might want to "own the airspace" around Burger King locations. Target might want to advertise at Walmart stores. Nissan might want to advertise to people at Toyota dealerships.

Geo-conquesting, while not widely used today, offers the promise of having a significant impact for advertisers. One of the comparisons I frequently draw is between geo-conquesting and retargeting. Advertisers always buy retargeting because it performs so well, yet their spend is constrained by the amount of visitors that they receive. If I was able to offer advertisers the ability to retarget people that went to competitor web sites, they would love it. They would spend as much as they could on it. Consider Ford Motor Company: Given the chance would they love to target people that had gone to the GM web site? Of course they would. The performance would probably not be as amazing as showing ads to people who came to the Ford web site, but targeting people at the GM web site is the essence of true advertising: The chance to change people's minds about what brands they are considering purchasing!

If competitive retargeting is conceptually a slam dunk (while being in practice impossible; GM would never let Ford pixel their web site and cookie their users), then geo-conquesting makes just as much sense. Wouldn't Ford want to reach people that have expressed interest in GM products in the same way?

I recently heard a speech by a senior marketing executive at Chrysler where they complained about the performance of their geo-conquesting campaigns relative to geo-fencing their own dealers. I found it dismaying that the value of reaching people who where not previously pre-disposed toward their brand was so easily dismissed. Changing minds is hard, but doing so is probably the most rewarding thing a marketer can do.

Further, geo-conquesting is always available. It is very difficult to "own" all of the inventory associated with your physical locations. This is much more difficult than buying a brand keyword on Google. Also, geo-conquesting is something that can be combined with location-based or content-based behavioral targeting to segment and optimize different populations. By discovering high performing pockets of geo-conquestable inventory, an advertiser can create tremendous value for their business.

Behavioral Location Targeting

The power of location targeting can be used in other ways as well: To extend a behavioral targeting metaphor to location. Consider this: In the same way that I can build a behavioral model in the digital world based on the sites you visit, I can build a similar model in the physical world based on the places you go. People that visit Yahoo! Finance three times in one week might be considered Finance Junkies. Similarly, someone that visits McDonalds three times in one week might be considered a Fast Food Lover.[22]

Many of the same kinds of concepts of targeting found in digital behavioral targeting have location-based corollaries. For example, digital retargeting shows ads to people that visit your web site. In mobile advertising, one can target ads to people that have been seen at a physical location in the past. This ability to model a population creates exciting opportunities for advertisers, particularly retailers that value location data above other kinds of data sets.

Cross-Device Targeting

As mobile has exploded, one of the most fascinating trends has been the emergence of omni-screen or cross-device targeting.

---

22. I am too kind to call them junkies!

With an abundance of registration data, device location data, and other data points, it is possible to identify as a consumer moves from their smartphone to their tablet to their desktop and use the data from each to supplement the individual siloed data sets and build more robust user information.

A recent study by the ANA indicated that the percentage of media budgets dedicated to multiscreen advertising is expected to rise from 20% this year to 50% during the next three years.[10] While the report defined multiscreen campaigns as those that run during a similar time frame across two or more screens, obviously a large and growing percentage will be using targeting mechanisms that take advantage of multiscreen but reach a similar audience. Bob Lord, the head of Aol Advertising, recently said that more than 45% of his clients display advertising spend was cross-screen[11].

Cross-device targeting is most simple for large portals that have dedicated apps and large bases of registered users. When someone logs into the Gmail app from their phone and then logs in to gmail.com on their desktop, it is elementary for Google to tie together the smartphone and the desktop device and recognize that this is a single user. It is more challenging for non-portals, but still possible.

Many techniques involve using location data and network data to identify home locations ("householding") for the user. For example, the home location might be the location where this user is seen late in the evenings most days of the week. If you can identify a home location for a desktop based on networking data and then identify mobile devices that are using the same home network, it seems reasonable to be able to tie these data sets together.

This creates a wide variety of behavioral and retargeting opportunities for advertisers which is particularly exciting in the mobile industry – they can suddenly sell behaviors from the desktop that advertisers are already comfortable buying providing incremental reach to advertisers.

Advertising companies like Drawbridge, TapAd, and Verve and fingerprinting specialists such as AdTruth specialize in such technologies that look at time of use, content patterns, and other data sets to create a probabilistic model matching multiple devices together. Similarly, because iOS doesn't support third party cookies, the same technology may be useful to map cookies on a device to the device ID of the mobile app usage connecting a user's disparate activities across the same device together.

The obvious question that arises from this is what kind of effective match rates the industry might see based on this. If we are using algorithms that model these behaviors, there is a probability that these matches are wrong - or, more accurately stated, a certainty that a percentage of these matches are wrong.

The industry claims that they believe there is a 50%-80% effective match rate for the industry specialists today, but many industry leaders imply that the best way to discern the effectiveness of the match is to look at campaign performance[12]. The implication that campaigns perform well due to high match rates seems potentially specious. As we have noted, low match rates would expand the pool of targetable individuals allowing for other kinds of optimization. It is unlikely that simply looking at campaign performance sheds light on the effectiveness of matching today.

Furthermore, the real underlying message here is that there is a degree of "waste" in the campaign that is fairly significant. 20% to 50% of the campaign is reaching the wrong audience. While no probabilistic approach can be expected to near 100%, partnering with people that have approaches that seem likely to have higher match rates seem important to the legitimate success of omni-screen targeting.

Notes

1. Shamdasani, PremN., Andrea J. S. Stanaland and Juliana Tan (2001), "Location, Location,
Location: Insightsfor Advertising Placement on the Web," Journal of Advertising Research, 41
(4), 7-21.
2.
http://anzmac.info/conference/2007/papers/R%20Hussain_2a.pdf
3.
http://www.iab.net/about_the_iab/recent_press_releases/press_release_archive/press_release/pr-062410
4. http://www.slideshare.net/Recrue/retargeting-performance-brief-4635689
5.
http://journals.ama.org/doi/abs/10.1509/jmr.11.0503?journalCode=jmkr
6. http://adexchanger.com/data-exchanges/kraft-exec-programmatic-is-a-centerpiece-for-us/
7. GSMA, World Bank, Enders Analysis
8. http://i2.ypcdn.com/radiant/radiant_assets_47482_YP-Local-Insights-Q3.pdf
9. http://www.vervemobile.com/pdfs/verve_retail_report_w.pdf
10. http://www.adexchanger.com/online-advertising/ana-survey-half-of-media-budgets-will-be-multiscreen-in-three-years/

---

11. http://www.adexchanger.com/mobile/tackling-cross-device-recognition-targeting/

12.   http://www.adexchanger.com/data-exchanges/the-cross-device-question-turn/

http://www.adexchanger.com/mobile/have-the-accuracy-rates-of-probabilistic-solutions-hit-a-glass-ceiling/

CHAPTER 13

Conclusion

Recently, I spent some time with a startup that had just raised about $1 million in funding for their consumer ecommerce marketplace and they were struggling to reach their new subscriber goals. When I talked with them about what they were doing on the marketing front, they were testing many initiatives. They were running a retargeting campaign on AdRoll (a popular retargeting ad network) and Google, they were running a search campaign on Google, they had Facebook campaigns running, and they had recently purchased a sponsorship on a well-known publisher site in their field. When I reviewed their efforts, a number of things jumped out at me that I hope reading this book has taught you.

First, in their analytics, the only number they tracked was the cost per new marketplace member. By this metric, Google search was their worst performing marketing tool, yet they continued to invest heavily in Google because they suspected (without data) that these marketplace members were their biggest revenue generators. Obviously, to the extent they find it a justification to invest, they should track this metric. Further, in this situation I would recommend assigning a value to new users and then co-mingling the metrics for new user growth and revenue. It could be that a company is at a stage where they place a premium on user growth, in which case they would place a premium value on a user. As the company matures, they could lower that value. While you want to track each value separately and monitor them over time, a co-mingled value allows you to easily arrive at a single number that tells you how each channel is doing and allows you to globally optimize in a straightforward way.

Second, while they had new subscriber goals and they knew what their costs were for each platform, they had not done the simple math to tell them how much they should be willing to pay for a subscriber.

Third, they co-mingled the results from various targeting types by rolling it up to a single platform. So their primary report was a report they generated weekly that showed this performance with a line item for Google, AdRoll, Facebook, and their publisher partner. Unfortunately, because things like Google contained several different targeting mechanisms, the effectiveness of each individual mechanism was obscured.

Digging into all of this data revealed opportunities to find additional value in Google by looking for far more keywords than they had been targeting and opportunities for additional value in retargeting by testing better creative messages. It also revealed that the markets they were bidding in experienced significant fluctuations. They would find from week to week that the places they put more money to work in rapidly became their most expensive acquisition channel, demonstrating that incremental conversions had higher price points. They needed to actually look at snapshots of the data daily and re-budget to maximize the value they were getting out of their daily spend.

Their last growth undertaking was the most challenging; they had embarked on an extremely expensive one-month sponsorship of a topical publishers site. They were one week into the sponsorship and were only seeing about one-tenth of the traffic and conversions that the publisher had told them they would expect. They weren't sure what to do. My answer was simple: Cancel the buy. Their initial response was that the publisher told them that they had cut the rate for this sponsorship in half already so they were getting a really good deal and also that there would be some embarrassment associated with calling the publisher to cancel. It felt like confessing to failure.

My response to this was simple: With respect to the "deal" the publisher offered, it may have been a good deal, but if it isn't performing well for you, then it isn't that great a deal. A good deal is a deal where you would pay more for the performance you are getting, but you don't have to. This is a bad deal that could have been even worse. They are the ones that should feel embarrassed by their failure to deliver.

Smart publishers will try to negotiate or offer to optimize to achieve higher performance. My suggestion to you is that this is your chance to shift terms to paying only for performance. If they think they can do better, you should only pay if they do.

Finally, while this is all interesting and good, they run a marketplace. The metrics they used were top of the funnel and bottom of the funnel and little else. The result was that it was difficult to tell how effective their marketing was with respect to Activation, Retention, and Referral.

Digital advertising continues to evolve at a breakneck pace. As attribution improves and the focus on efficiency increases, the growth of real-time bidding should continue to grow and spread to every aspect of digital advertising. As the CFO of Rocket Fuel (a popular DSP), Peter Barthwick, put it:

"I expect programmatic to slow down in the same way people stopped trading on exchanges and went back to handing pieces of paper back and forth for selling stocks."[1]

This allows each business and participant in the market to establish their own value proposition based on the value of their data and their algorithms.

Startups need more than growth hacking to take their business through product market fit. Besides an amazing product and an effective viral loop, lean start-ups need to effectively acquire both organic traffic and develop scalable ROI-driven platforms for customer acquisition. By executing and investing in every aspect of Acquisition, Activation, Retention, Referral, and Revenue, the Lifetime Customer Value of users can be maximized and growth of the business can be optimized.

As part of customer discovery, you should be identifying what kind of growth engine your start-up will use and begin laying the appropriate groundwork to scale the business effectively using machines, people and cash.

Innovation is the starting point for every great business, but without a strong program for enabling marketing and sales, that innovation is wasted. If you are building a business using growth by SEO, virality, paid customer acquisition, or even a sales force, you will find that the mix of techniques outlined will give you the tools to launch, measure, and refine these techniques to ensure the success of your start-up.

Notes

1. http://www.adexchanger.com/platforms/achieving-liftoff-in-a-world-of-disruption-rocket-fuel-ceo-cfo-ignite-a-fireside-chat/#more-85449

ABOUT THE AUTHOR

Brent Halliburton lives in Washington D.C. with his wife, two children and a dog

KEEP READING

This is Brent Halliburton's first book, but that doesn't mean the reading has to stop here. His web site, http://brenthalliburton.com is chock-full of digital goodies.

Alternately, you can follow him:

Twitter: http://twitter.com/bhalliburton

Blog: http://brenthalliburton.com/

Made in the USA
Charleston, SC
24 February 2016